KRESGE
ADM.
ARY

D0365166

KRESGE
BUS. ADM.
LIBRARY

ECONOMIC POLICY AFTER 1992

ECONOMIC POLICY AFTER 1992

Edited by
D.H. Gowland
and
S. James

Dartmouth

Aldershot • Brookfield USA • Hong Kong • Sydney

Bus Adm
HC
241.2
.E165

© D.H.Gowland and S. James 1991

All rights reserved. No part of this publication may be reproduced, stored in a retrieval system, or transmitted in any form or by any means, electronic, mechanical, photocopying, recording, or otherwise without the prior permission of Dartmouth Publishing Company Limited.

Published by
Dartmouth Publishing Company Limited
Gower House
Croft Road
Aldershot
Hants GU11 3HR

Dartmouth Publishing Company
Old Post Road
Brookfield
Vermont 05036
USA

British Library Cataloguing in Publication Data
Economic policy after 1992.
   1. Europe. Economic conditions. Policies
   I. Gowland, David II. James, Stephen
   338.941

Library of Congress Cataloging-in-Publication Data
Economic policy after 1992 / edited by David Gowland and
   Stephen James.
     p. cm.
   ISBN 1-85521-205-6 : $55.95 (U.S. : est.)
    1. European Economic Community countries–Economic policy.
   2. Economic forecasting–European Economic Community countries.
   3. Europe 1992. I. Gowland, David II. James, Stephen
   HC241.2.E2934 1991
   338.94'001'12–dc20

ISBN 1 85521 205 6

90-27520
CIP

Printed in Great Britain by
Billing & Sons Ltd, Worcester
Laserset by Computype Manuscript Services, Standard House, 49 Lawrence Street, York

A 43649
0-21-92

Contents

OCT 2 3 1992 ✓

Contributors

sect c 8 730

Theodore Georgakopoulos is a Professor of the academic staff at the Athens University of Economics and Business.

David Gowland is a lecturer in Economics and Director of In-Service Courses at the University of York. He formerly worked in the Bank of England and the Policy Unit, 10 Downing Street. He is author of various books including *Regulation of Financial Markets,* Edward Elgar, 1990.

Keith Hartley is a Professor of Economic Policy and Director of the Centre for Defence Econoics at the University of York. He is the author of various books including the *Regulation of Financial Markets,* Edward Elgar, 1990.

Theo Hitiris is a Senior Lecturer in Economics at the University of York. He is the author of many books and articles including *European Community Economics,* Harvester-Wheatsheaf, 2nd edition 1990.

Stephen James is a lecturer at Teeside Business School. He is the author of various articles and is a member of SEAC Working Parties on Business Studies and Economics After and GCSE After 1994.

Andrew Jones is a lecturer in Economics at the University of York. His main research interests are in the economics of consumer behaviour and taxation.

Giovanni Palmerio is Rittore of the University of Molise, Campobasso and Director of the Institute of Economic Studies at LUISS, Rome.

1 Economic policy after *1992*: introduction

Stephen James

"This large market without frontiers, because of its size and because of the possibilities that it offers for scientific, technical and commercial co-operation, gives a unique opportunity to our industry to improve our competitivity. It will also increase growth and employment and contribute to a better balance in the world economy ... It is revolutionary, but it will be achieved both because it is absolutely necessary and because it carries with it the goal of a united and strong Europe" (Jacques Delors in Cecchini, 1988).

"(1992) should be treated with the intelligent scepticism which should be applied to any marketing campaign. The images and slogans of the advertisement should not be confused with reality ... The significance of *1992* is almost entirely to be found in measures which are industry-specific" (Kay, 1989).

Anyone who has not heard of the EC's *1992* Single Market initiative must either be impervious to modern propaganda techniques or have lived the life of a hermit – perhaps not an unenviable existence. As John Kay (1989) has said, it is probably one of the most successful marketing campaigns of the 1980s and this after the immense privatisation hype in the UK in the same decade. Naturally perceptions differ widely as the above quotations indicate. They range from the hyperbole of the euro-zealots such as Jacque Delors to the more measured, even cynical tones of John Kay.

The objective of this introductory discussion is to examine the *1992* proposals, to consider the possible effects of the Single Market programme and to indicate some of the implications it has for the conduct of economic policy in the EC

1.1 THE *1992* PROGRAMME IN OUTLINE

To the enthusiast the *1992* programme represents a cure-all for the parlous state into which the European economy fell in the 1970s and the first half of the 1980s. The simultaneous appearance of high inflation and unemployment, the decline in the rate of economic growth and the productivity slowdown were all seen as symptoms of the same disease – Eurosclerosis. Fears mounted that Europe was increasingly falling behind the world's leading economies, the US and Japan, in competitiveness and technological leadership. *1992*, therefore, represents an attempt to administer a supply-side shock to the European economy that will:

a) produce a once-and-for-all increase in GDP and
b) induce dynamic changes that will permanently raise growth rates.

It should be noted that there is some divergence in the experience of the separate EC economies; contrast for example the recent economic history of the UK and West Germany. Furthermore, similar economic problems beset other economies, for example, the US, and produced not dissimilar calls for urgent remedial action. Whilst there is ample evidence to suggest that Europe's economies had become increasingly inflexible (see Boltho, 1982; Lawrence and Schultz, 1987), the 1970s and 1980s were marked by major supply-side shocks and a macroeconomic environment less than conducive to growth. Indeed, a return to a rather more settled state of affairs in the later 1980s has produced a marked improvement in EC economic performance, although unemployment rates remain persistently high in a number of countries, for example Italy and France.

2

Other factors also explain the enthusiasm with which the *1992* idea has been taken up. The wranglings over the budget contributions and the inward-looking, protective industrial policies pursued by EC governments during the early '80s recession (Pearce and Sutton 1986) seemed to sap the momentum of any drive for European unity, be it political or economic. The slowness of the progress towards integration also caused some concern after the initial impetus given by the formation, and later expansions, of the Common Market had faded. The process slowed towards the end of the 1970s and indeed by the early 1980s seemed to have come to a halt as protectionism gained a hold. *1992* as a result represented a new focus for the united Europe ideal as can be seen from the headnote quotation from Jacques Delors. This has been added to by the success of the EMS in bringing about macroeconomic policy co-ordination amongst those countries participating in the exchange rate mechanism and by the convergence in their inflation rates. Finally, the particular emphasis of the *1992* proposals on the freeing of trade across all markets within the EC reflects a greater acceptance of the importance of market forces and a shift away from a direct interventionist philosophy.

Set out in the EC Commission White Paper "Completing the Internal Market" (EC 1985) and the Single European Act (effective from 1/7/1987), the objective of the *1992* programme is to create a single European market for goods, services, labour and capital. Strictly speaking of course it should be a single EC market – there are more than 12 countries in Europe. Essentially it consists of dismantling the remaining barriers to trade between EC countries. These are entirely non-tariff restrictions; the tariff barriers between the original six were removed progressively over a ten year transition period (1958-68) and for the three 1973 entrants (UK, Denmark and Ireland) between 1973 and 1978.

Following the Commission, the barriers to be removed can be grouped into three rather broad categories; physical, technical and fiscal:[1]

Physical
These refer to frontier controls such as physical checks and paperwork and quotas on goods. There are also others on the agenda including transport restrictions such as quotas on foreign hauliers operating in EC countries and limitations on the free movement of people. The intention of the *1992* measures is to remove these barriers completely.

3

Technical

These barriers cover a host of other trade restrictions from health and safety regulations and technical standard on products to the recognition of workers' qualifications in different EC countries and the different regulatory systems for services, especially financial services. Other aspects include legal differences such as on company law and the restrictions on EC wide competition in the important area of public procurement. The intention of the Single Market programme is to open up EC countries markets by standardisation or mutual recognition and to liberalise public procurement.

Fiscal

The principal barriers here are the widely varying rates of VAT and excise duty. The Commission proposes some degree of harmonisation of VAT rates into two bands (4 – 9 per cent and 15 per cent plus with some zero rating continuing) and complete harmonisation of excise duties. The main reasons are to prevent cross border shopping and to support the dismantling of the frontier controls. For the latter reason the VAT tax refund system on exports is to be changed. At the time of writing (September 1990) there has been little progress in the area of income and other direct taxation except perhaps in the taxation of financial capital (see Georgakopoulos and Hitiris, p.143).

In their assessment of the Single Market proposals Pelkmans and Winters (1988) classify the *1992* measures into four categories according to the effects they will have. These are: improving market access, increasing competition, measures dealing with market failure and measures relating to specific sectoral policy (for example steel). They are non-exclusive, and the first three are useful to us in assessing the effects of *1992*.

By and large the emphasis of *1992* is to improve market access and this explains the concentration on removing frontier controls and technical restrictions on goods and services, capital and labour. It is hoped that the outcome of this will be enhanced competition in many instances as firms gain greater access to wider European markets. In some markets, however, access *per se,* though necessary, is not sufficient. This explains the need for competition measures in, for example, public procurement and also the proposals to restrict state aid to industries – though "with substantial exceptions" – and proposals for

4

common policies on mergers. Improvements in the functioning of markets and dealing with market failure may entail inter-country harmonisations in areas such as patent laws and technical standard, pollution control and a number of others.

Taken together the measures are designed to create, in the EC jargon, a unified or integrated market across the Community in which trade across national frontiers is unrestricted. The implication for businesses and consumers is that they should widen their horizons beyond their own national customers or supplies. The concept of a single market, however, is a very misleading one. Indeed, Europe will continue to be a series of local, national or international markets for different goods and services, the scope being determined by the supply and demand conditions within each market (see Kay 1989). The importance of the policies to improve market access and increase competition within the EC lies in the fact that they break down the *artificial* barriers to trade that separate national markets when there are no economic reasons for doing so. There is, on the other hand, no logical reason why distinct markets, which may be local, regional or national, separated by natural barriers should not continue to remain. Given the rich cultural and linguistic diversity of the existing twelve countries of the Community, not to mention the far greater diversity that will arise from any future expansions of the EC, it seems rather misleading, if not a little trite, to talk of a single market in Europe. This is considered more fully below in the chapter on Industrial Policy (p.29–30).

1.2 THE EFFECTS OF *1992*: AN ECONOMIC FRAMEWORK

The removal of the non-tariff barriers can be analysed within a simple economic framework. *1992* provides five sources of gain to the EC economies, four static and one dynamic.

1.2.1 Improved allocation

The basic gain in economic welfare from the removal of trade barriers can be demonstrated by the use of a graph (Figure 1) which illustrates the position of country Y. As a small country in the EC market it faces a horizontal supply curve for imports of product X. Assuming that frontier controls in Y raise the price of imports of X by 25 per cent above the EC price, the price of X is P_1, demand is X_1, home supply X_2 and imports are $X_1 - X_2$. Removal of the frontier controls reduces the price of imports to P_2 by shifting down the import supply curve to S_2, raising home consumption to X_3, though at the cost of a fall in home production to X_4 and a rise in imports to $X_3 - X_4$. This produces a welfare gain given by the increase in consumers' surplus $A + B + C + D$, which is offset only by the loss in economic rent to home producers (A). This leaves a net gain of $B + C + D$ which is made up of:

(i) The net savings in resources by purchasing $X_2 - X_4$ of good X from abroad more cheaply than it could be produced at home (B)

(ii) The savings on resources used up in frontier controls (C)

(iii) The deadweight gain in consumers' surplus resulting from increased consumption (D). It is interesting to note that the net gain from the removal of a non-tariff trade barrier such as a frontier control exceeds that from the reduction in a tariff that has an equivalent protective effect. This is because the abolition of the frontier controls give rise to a resource saving of C whereas in the tariff case C would represent a loss in tariff revenue and therefore a redistribution of income.

1.2.2 Cost reductions

Improving market access and intensifying competitive pressures increase the incentive on firms to adopt cost minimising production processes. Consequently X – inefficiency falls, lowering prices, raising output and releasing resources for use in other sectors of the economy. In the field of public procurement greater EC-wide competition and the abandoning of the 'national champion' approach to industrial policy may also produce savings in public expenditure.

1.2.3 Erosion of monopoly power

The traditional welfare case against monopoly power is that at the margin the price consumers are willing to pay exceeds marginal cost. Output could be raised and yield positive net benefits to society. The ending of protection of domestic monopolies and greater competition in the domestic market pushes prices down and outputs towards their optimum levels.

6

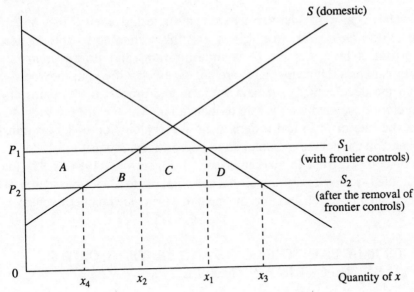

Figure 1.1

1.2.4 Economies of scale

The advent of a larger market – of over 320 million people, in *1992* marketing jargon – will enable firms to take advantage of hitherto unexploited economies of scale, with consequent reductions in unit costs and expansion in output. The net welfare gain is shown by shifting the MC curve downwards and to the right (see Gowland, 1982, p.179). In addition there may well be reductions in unit costs arising from learning effects of long production runs.

The benefits from economies of scale, however, are problematic. Their realisation may conflict with the objective of increased competition and it is not altogether evident, either on the basis of reasoning or empirical evidence, that the benefits of large scale production are available across the broad mass of European industries. The benefits are likely to be limited to a few sectors (see Chapter 2 on Industrial Policy).

1.2.5 Dynamic gains

The above gains all refer to improvements in technical efficiency and in the allocation of resources given existing technology – production approaches best practice (cost minimisation) and prices approach marginal costs. Dynamic gains are not easily classified but they derive from the developments of new products and processes; the gains are therefore dependent on the rate of innovation. Much evidence suggests that the rate of technical progress and the exploitation of innovations depend on the degree of competition (Geroski and Jacquemin, 1985). A more competitive EC market is seen by Cecchini (1988, p.85) for example, as providing a much needed impetus to a virtuous circle of European innovation and improvement in worldwide competitiveness.

1.3 ESTIMATES OF THE COSTS AND BENEFITS, OR THE CECCHINI REPORT IN A NUTSHELL[2]

The official EC estimate of the gain from the completion of the single market is put at around ECU 200 billion at 1988 prices or 5 per cent of the EC Gross Domestic Product in 1988. The consumer price level is anticipated to be around 6 per cent lower. This is based on unchanged macroeconomic policies. A higher estimate is derived when policy is more expansionary: GDP is 7 per cent higher and five million new jobs are created. Conversely, these estimates can be taken as the costs of maintaining the barriers.

The Cecchini Report (Cecchini 1988) attempts to measure the benefits of competition in four ways:

1.3.1 Estimating the costs of the existing barriers

Rather ungracefully this is known as the costs of 'non-Europe'. Based on the 13 specialist reports on multi-sector barriers, barriers in the service industries and in manufacturing, the Commission estimated the costs of delays and administration imposed on traders operating across national boundaries. They also included the resource costs of operating the barriers. Some of the findings are documented in Tables 1.1 and 1.2. The results show that border control costs amounted to 1.6 to 1.7 per cent of community trade; other evidence indicates that the incidence was not distributed evenly between firms or industries or that the administrative costs were the same in different EC countries. Small firms were the most seriously affected as were the engineering, precision and medical equipment sectors and pharmaceuticals. The administrative costs to firms were greatest in Italy and lowest in Belgium (see Table 1.3).

Table 1.1
Costs of multi-sector barriers

Border controls	Cost (ECUm)	
Administration	7,500	
Delays	415–830	12,915
Business forgone	4,500–1,500	to 24,330
Spending on customs checks	500–1,000	
Public procurement	17,500	
Technical regulations and standards	"Costs difficult to quantify but impossible to ignore" 8,586 (covers Telecoms, Foodstuffs, Building and Motor Vehicles)	
Trans-border business	"difficult to quantify, ... in terms of tens of billions of ECU."	

Source: Cecchini, 1988

Pharmaceuticals can be taken to illustrate the effects of the controls. In this industry there are two principle barriers to market entry: the strict system of price controls in most countries and the need to meet separate registration requirements in each country. As regards the costs of multiple registration this can be broken down into three main areas: the requirement for additional staff (40–55 million ECU), registration delays resulting in capital being tied-up (20–28 million ECU) and the impact of delays in reducing the effective duration of patents. These delays can be for two years or more and will reduce the sales revenues of the pharmaceutical companies (100–175 million ECU). Price and profit controls which are often related to discrimination in favour of domestic

9

firms may benefit the public budget but have the adverse effects of limiting competition and possibly reducing the scope for economies of scale. It is reported by the Commission that, as a result of steps towards integration, and a convergence of prices towards the EC average, there would be a saving of around 720 million ECU (Emerson, 1988, p.75).

Table 1.2
Costs of non-Europe, industry estimates

Services

Financial	ECU 22bn
Telecoms	ECU 4bn
Business services	ECU 9.2 bn

Manufacturing

Telecom equipment	ECU 3–4.8 bn
Motor cars	ECU 2.6 bn
Foods	ECU 500 million to 1 billion
Pharmaceuticals	ECU 160–248 m (Registration practices only)
Building	ECU 820 m (1.7 bn in the long term)
Textile and clothing	0.2–0.5 per cent of unit costs

Source: Cecchini, 1988

Table 1.3
Administrative costs of trade barriers to firms (ECU per consignment)

	Imports	*Exports*
Belgium	26	34
Germany	42	79
France	92	87
Italy	130	205
The Netherlands	46	50
United Kingdom	75	49
Average	67	86

Source: Emerson, 1988

1.3.2 Price convergence

In a fully integrated market arbitrage ensures that prices tend to converge. The table below (Table 1.4) shows, however, that in a good many products there is a significant dispersion of prices in EC markets indicating that hitherto there has been considerable market segmentation, limiting competition and market access. Steps towards market integration that raise competition will produce downward pressure on costs and prices and in the Commission's estimates will give rise to total savings in the region of 4.8 per cent of Community GDP (Cecchini, 1988, p.82). However, not all price differentials can be explained by artificial barriers; there may be natural ones such as transport costs or differences in consumers' preferences. Furthermore, the price convergence approach has a major drawback in that it assumes that GDP remains constant thus ignoring the stimulus to demand and output, and hence the full welfare gains of a price fall.

Table 1.4
Price divergence in E.C. countries (1985)

	Price divergence measured by coefficient of variation (%)[1]	
	Prices without indirect taxes	*Prices with indirect taxes*
Preserved milk	24.6	22.2
Edible oils	22.3	23.2
Potatoes	28.4	29.1
Coffee and cocoa	26.9	14.1
Beer	20.9	41.1
Non-alcoholic beverages	24.8	33.1
Ladies underclothing and knitwear	30.7	31.8
Motor vehicles	13.6	26.8
Radio sets and record players	15.5	18.9
Medicines and pharmaceuticals	32.6	33.3
Books	48.6	57.0
Jewellery and watches	22.0	24.6
Boilermaking products	22.1	–
Locomotives	21.7	–
Aircraft	17.1	–

Note.

1. Coefficient of variation (%) = $\dfrac{\text{Standard Deviation}}{\text{Mean}} \times 100$

(Source: Emerson, 1988)

1.3.3 Estimating the welfare gain

A more satisfactory approach than the price convergence one is to estimate the welfare gains resulting from the four main effects of the *1992* changes, that is, the reduction of trade barriers, the gains from increased competition, the reduction in monopoly power and the exploitation of economies of scale. This approach corresponds to the four main static gains noted in the previous section, and a breakdown of the benefits is given in Table 5 below. It is interesting to note that approximately one third of the gains accrue as a result of scale economies and one quarter from increased competition. The potential for conflict between these two effects must cast some doubt on the full realisation of the gains from these two sources (see Chapter 2).

Table 1.5
Estimated welfare gains from 1992

	Billions ECU	% of GDP
Step 1		
Gains from removal of barriers affecting trade	8–9	0.2–0.3
Step 2		
Gains from removal of barriers affecting overall production	57–71	2.0–2.4
Gains from removing barriers (sub-total)	65–80	2.2–2.7
Step 3		
Gains from exploiting economies of scale more fully	61	2.1
Step 4		
Gains from intensified competition reducing business inefficiencies and monopoly profits	46	1.6
Gains from market integration (sub-total)	62–107	2–3.7
Total		
– for 7 Member States at 1985 prices	127–187	4.3–6.4
– for 12 Member States at 1988 prices	174–258	4.3–6.4
– mid-point of above	216	5.3

Source: Cecchini, 1988

12

1.3.4 Estimating the macroeconomic effects

To give an alternative perspective the Cecchini team provided macroeconomic estimates, treating the *1992* programme essentially as a major supply-side shock to the EC economies. The effects can be stated in terms of a conventional *AS-AD* model. The reduction in trade barriers, greater liberalisation and intensified competition raises productivity and reduces costs, shifting the *AS* curve to the right. In addition, savings on public spending as procurement is opened up reduces tax burdens and interest rates, the latter encouraging investment in productive capacity, further adding to the beneficial supply shift. The result is higher output, lower unemployment and reduced inflation. The predicted effects are summarised in Table 6.

Table 1.6
The macroeconomic effects of 1992

	Customs formal- ities	Public procure- ment	Financial services	Supply- side effects[1]	Total Average value	Total Spread
Relative changes (%)						
GDP	0.4	0.5	1.5	2.1	4.5	(3.2–5.7)
Consumer prices	–1.0	–1.4	–1.4	–2.3	–6.1	(–4.5 – –7.7)
Absolute changes						
Employment (millions)	200	350	400	850	1800	(1300–2300)
Budgetary balance (% point of GDP)	0.2	0.3	1.1	0.6	2.2	(1.5–3.0)
External balance (% of point of GDP)	0.2	0.1	0.3	–0.4	1.0	(0.7–1.3)

Source: HERMES (EC Commission and national teams) and INTERLINK (OECD) economic models.

Note:
1. Based on a scenario which includes the supply-side effects estimated by the consultants, economies of scale in manufacturing industry and competition effects (monopoly rent, X-inefficiency).

Source: Cecchini, 1988

13

In each of these estimates the assessed benefits refer to once-and-for-all gains in economic efficiency in the years after the completion of the internal market programme. This is referred to by Cecchini as the medium-term, a period of up to about five years. Neither Cecchini nor the Commission's more detailed work provide estimates of any 'gear change' in the growth path of the EC economies over the long-term as a result of the greater spur to innovation and further technical progress. There can be little doubt, however, that the Commission regards the growth effects as important, if not more so, than the static gains. Richard Baldwin (1989) has attempted to quantify the growth effect: perhaps rather optimistically he suggests that *1992* may add between 0.2–0.9 per cent to the growth rate in Europe.

ECONOMIC POLICY AFTER *1992*

The success of the *1992* programme in improving living standards in the EC will depend to a large extent on the economic policy environment. The pursuit of inappropriate or contradictory policies by governments or the Commission, or the inefficient allocation of functions between the various policy making institutions could have the effect of offsetting the gains of the single market reforms. An important element in determining post-*1992* policy is the vision of the EC's future and the way in which the integration process will be managed. Here there are two distinct camps. On one side are the Continental visionaries who approach the integration of Europe and the strengthening of common institutions with immense fervour. In Italy economists such as Einaudi and Röpke have been influential in this respect. Their view is that the quicker the movement towards a federalist union of EC states the better and, moreover, this is best directed from the centre. On the other side are the sceptics from what may be termed the Anglo-Saxon school. While they are not necessarily opposed to the idea of a greater degree of European integration, economists of this persuasion are concerned both at its pace and the centralising potential of an enhanced Commission and other federalist institutions. Mrs Thatcher has expressed this in extreme form: "We have not destroyed socialism in Britain to recreate it in Brussels." To some extent the concerns are political but they are also economic: they include such matters as the freedom of governments to operate their own independent policies as well as the economic effects of large centralised bureaucracies, especially their market-distorting impact. For many reasons, therefore, the best route to economic (and political) integration is regarded as a slower, evolutionary one in which the steps towards common policies and institutions occurs as and when the need arises to solve particular problems. The approach has been variously dubbed the 'bottom-up' or 'Jeffersonian' model by Helm and Smith (1989) and Kay and Posner (1989) respectively.

One area in which the contrast is particularly evident is that of industrial policy. What is more, the policy response here is crucial since many of the gains from the *1992* measures are expected to come from the industrial sector. Thus the large market with improved access is seen as essential to the stimulation of increased competition and as an incentive to firms to restructure and achieve economies of scale. It is argued in Chapter 2, however, that not only are the estimated gains from scale economies open to question, but also that the very benefits from the competition-intensifying removal of non-tariff barriers could be undermined either by a tendency to a more interventionist policy at the EC level or by competitive industrial policies of national governments. As regards the latter, there is a clear case for EC-level policy, but one which seeks to ensure that governments play by the agreed Community rules. Some developments along these lines are currently occurring for instance on the stricter application of Community rules on industrial subsidies and in a common mergers policy. As far as an activist policy to promote 'European Champion' firms is concerned, the drawbacks should be clear in terms of the implications for the abuse of market power and the opportunities it provides for rent-seeking behaviour and bargaining with the EC for special concessions.

A surer way of obtaining the competition-enhancing advantages of the *1992* initiative is to improve the competitive pressures on European enterprises. Keith Hartley points out in Chapter 5 that the opening up of the public purchasing market will produce major benefits. For too long public procurement has been a way of featherbedding inefficient domestic businesses or promoting national champions, with undesirable consequences for the public budget and, possibly, on the quality of public sector services. There is also scope for some major restructuring. In boilermaking, turbine generators and locomotive producing industries for example, not only are there significant unrealised scale economies and a large number of European firms in the sectors but also fairly low degrees of capacity utilization (Emerson, 1988, p.54). Nevertheless, it remains to be seen whether there is the political will to open up these markets. The extensive privatisation in some countries such as the UK may well help in this respect but for countries with sizeable public sectors and a large number of important nationalised industries it still remains an option to support domestic firms, albeit by paying higher prices.

Another related field is that of trade policy, and some disquiet has been expressed, particularly in the US, over a possible Fortress Europe attitude to trade. It is clear that a frontierless internal market renders ineffective any attempt by individual countries to operate an independent commercial policy and, consequently, there may be some attempt to extend a number of the existing national quotas to the EC level. On the whole such fears seem to be without foundation at present. Protectionist trade policy can also operate in other ways such as through subsidies, as in the case of the Common Agricultural Policy. Another important one is the use of common EC standards that exclude external producers, or at least puts them at a disadvantage *vis à vis* European industry. For example, attempts to create a deregulated and competitive telecommunications market in Europe by setting a common standard has been interpreted in the US as a protective measure (see Huntley, Pitt and Trauth, 1990). It may well be that in this case there is a genuine clash between increased European competition on the one hand and between Europe and the rest of the world on the other, but in general an open trade policy is likely to be the appropriate adjunct to the attempts to raise competitive pressure within Europe's internal market.

The deregulation of finance also has major implications for the conduct of economic policy. As David Gowland points out in Chapter 3, on the macroeconomic side the choice of the regulatory framework is problematic. Mutual recognition along with host country regulation could prove to be detrimental to consumers rather than producing the beneficial competitive results that the proponents of competing regulatory systems claim. Thus a reduction in the quality of financial services may occur as countries compete in the laxity of their regulations to attract lucrative financial services businesses.

The other area in which the *1992* reforms have set about levelling the European playing field is in the area of taxation. It was noted above that little progress has been made in the steps towards the harmonisation of direct taxes but, apart from those on corporations and financial capital or income derived from it, there seems to be little need for any urgency to press ahead with the harmonisation of income tax rates or social security arrangements. Labour is likely to remain relatively immobile for some time to come; in contrast, capital and businesses (especially financial) are much more mobile and therefore a stronger case can be made for harmonisation, or at least co-ordination in these areas. It is in indirect taxation that harmonization has been most vigorously pursued. As in other areas there are some disagreements over the extent to which harmonisation is either desirable or necessary; they are surveyed by Andrew Jones in Chapter 4. For now it is sufficient to mention just two important aspects. First, the application of the destination principle (that is, taxation in the country of sale not that of production) does not necessarily imply a need for the equalisation of tax rates as divergent rates are unlikely to affect the pattern of trade or production except perhaps in border areas. What harmonisation along current EC lines may do, however, is raise the administrative costs as revenues will have to be transferred between countries through a clearing system. Second, there are a number of countries that either stand to lose significant tax revenues from the harmonisation of excise duties or where there will be major changes in rates on such sensitive goods as alcohol products and tobacco to bring them into line. The problems in tax harmonisation have resulted in slow progress and led Kay and Posner (1989) to comment that:

"The evolution of fiscal policy has been characterised by the problem that since there is little (or no) prospect of action on harmonising things which are important, energy is then devoted to things which are not, with results that do little for the reputation of the Community or the cause of European integration." (p.61)

David Gowland in Chapter 3 also points out that financial deregulation also has very serious implications for the conduct of macroeconomic policy. While there are currently severe limitations on a country's ability to pursue a wholly independent macro policy, within Europe after *1992* it could well become a thing of the past: it certainly will under full monetary integration. With the freeing of capital movements and a fixed exchange rate system – or at least an adjustable peg – interest rates in any one EC country will be essentially tied to the European level. Moreover, manipulation of the budget for stabilisation purposes will not provide governments with any further latitude in the macroeconomic sphere, particularly with interest rates already determined. It is partly for these reasons that so much emphasis has been placed on the EC budget as well as a European central bank. Georgakopoulos and Hitiris indicate in their Chapter 5 that as (or if) the EC moves progressively towards economic and monetary union the EC budget will have to take in a macroeconomic stabilization role. This will not only require an increase in "own-resources" – EC funds that are not dependent on the contributions of member governments – but also a clear statement of how budgetary policy is to work. In neither area has there been much advance.

The other important function of the budget is to promote intra-Community equity by acting as a means through which the gains from the *1992* programme and economic integration are redistributed to the losers. It is not at all clear how the gains and losses will be distributed although there appear to be two alternative views on the subject. One is that the peripheral areas such as Southern Italy will lose out as industry migrates towards the 'core' of the European economy, that is, towards the France-Germany-Benelux areas. Under such circumstances there will be significant pressure for a transfer of resources to these poorer, outlying regions both in the form of direct industrial support and also through infrastructure investment. Such a policy is advocated by Giovanni Palmerio in Chapter 7. An alternative perspective is provided by Nevin (1990) who, in his examination of comparative advantage and intra-industry trade, suggests that significant gains will accrue to the poorer, Southern economies which will benefit from lower labour costs and the realisation of economies of scale. The principle beneficiaries are Portugal, Greece and possibly Spain. The gains to the Northern economies, which derive from intra-industry trade, are rather less marked since they are already well integrated and there is not so much scope for further scale economies. Nevertheless, irrespective of the outcome in the medium- or long-term, regional policy will be an area in which there is increasing emphasis.

NOTES

1. The *1992* programme originally consisted of 300 barrier removing measures that are due to be implemented by 1st January 1993. Negotiation between governments has reduced these; the current count is 286 (July 1990).
2. The Cecchini Report (1988) is a summary of the detailed studies of the effects of the Internal Market programme that is published as Emerson (1988).

REFERENCES

Baldwin, R. (1989) 'The Growth Effects of *1992*', *Economic Policy*, No.9.

Boltho, A. (ed.) (1982) *The European Economy: Growth and Crisis*, Oxford University Press.

Cecchini, P. (1988) *1992: The European Challenge*, Wildwood House.

Commission (1985) *Completing the Internal Market*, Com.(85) 310, Brussels.

Emerson, M. (1988) *The Economics of 1992*, Oxford University Press.

Geroski, P. and Jacquemin, A. (1985) 'Industrial Change, Barriers to Mobility and European Industrial Policy', *Economic Policy*, Vol.1, No.1.

Gowland, D.H. (1982) *Modern Economic Analysis 2*, Butterworths.

Helm, D. and Smith, S. (1989) 'Economic Integration and the Role of the European Community', *Oxford Review of Economic Policy*, Vol.5, No.2.

Hartley, J.A.K., Pitt, D.C. and Trauth, E. (1990), 'Post Fortressism – Trade, Telecommunications and the New Europe', *Proceedings of the European Trade and Technology Conference*, Sunderland Polytechnic, Sept. 1990.

Jacquemin, A. and Sapir, A. (1990) *The European Internal Market: Trade and Competition – Selected Readings*, Oxford University Press.

Kay, J.A. (1989) 'Myths and Realities', in E.H. Davis et al (1988) *1992: Myths and Realities*, Centre for Business Strategy, London Business School.

Kay, J.A. and Posner, M.V. (1989) ;Routes to Economic Integration: *1992* in the European Community', *National Institute Economic Review*, No.129.

Lawrence, R.Z. and Schultze, C.L. (1987) *Barriers to European Growth: A Transatlantic view*, extract reprinted in Jacquemin and Sapir (1990).

Pelkmans, J. and Winters, A. (1988) *European Domestic Market*, Chatham House Papers, No.43, RIAA/Routledge.

Pearce, J. and Sutton, J. (1986) *Protection and Industrial Policy in Europe*, RIAA/Routledge.

Nevin, D.J. (1990) 'Gains and Losses from *1992*', *Economic Policy*, Vol.5, No.1.

2 Industrial policy after *1992*: making the most of the internal market

Stephen James

2.1 INTRODUCTION

In the eyes of many enthusiasts the Single Market programme provides an ideal opportunity for European industry to regain competitive ground it has lost to the Japanese, the Americans and some fast growing newly industrialised countries. An important determinant of the effects of *1992* on the response of firms is the behaviour of national governments and the EC Commission in the field of industrial policy. One option that has been widely canvassed is for the Commission to pursue an activist policy towards European industry. This would entail the identification and promotion of designated growth sectors in addition to support for the vulnerable, maturer industries. In essence it would involve a transplantation of the French *dirigiste* style of industrial policy to the EC level but operating on a grander scale. In some areas, such as in the development of high-definition television this already appears to have begun. Since 1986 the Commission has subsidised and encouraged the joint efforts of the two main European television producers – Philips and Thomson – to produce their own exclusively European system. It is incompatible with the existing Japanese system. Of course, whether such a policy provides any long-term protection for the European market is debatable. Given the Japanese penchant for finding chinks in the protective armour, this type of European Champion approach may be both unwise as well as unsuccessful. The alternative, at the other end of the spectrum, is to follow the market approach that has traditionally been adopted in West Germany and by the U.K. Government from 1979 onwards. This emphasises the rigours of liberalised markets and the benefits of private ownership and initiative. The question of which of these two industrial policy regimes will help produce the desired boost to industrial efficiency in the wake of *1992* is the subject of much of this chapter.

More generally, the importance of *1992* for industrial policy is twofold: first, individual governments' policies will become increasingly, possibly severely constrained. To take just one example, that of subsidies to industry, the Commission's current view is that since these confer competitive advantages on domestic producers, they may well distort competition. Subsidisation will, therefore, come under far greater EC scrutiny than in the past (this issue is discussed at greater length below). The corollary of this is that the EC will play an increasingly important role in the area of industrial policy.

Second, there is the major question of the form that EC-level involvement in industrial policy will, and indeed should, take. In the most general terms this question concerns the degree to which industrial policy actions should be centralised, increasingly coming within the ambit of the Commission and the Council, with policy measures having EC-wide application. The alternative course is to permit member governments to retain significant freedom to operate their own policies. As noted, complete freedom, though constrained in the past, will become ever more so: the main point is the extent to which policy making will shift and government freedom curtailed. A related issue is the extent to which EC institutions, particularly the Commission, should play an active role in initiating policy or whether it would be best to take the field as a referee. A vigorously interventionist EC-wide policy would cast the Commission very much as an active participant in promoting European industry – "batting for Europe" to adapt Margaret Thatcher's phrase. A more free market approach is much more consistent with the refereeing role, though not exclusively so. There may be situations where active market-based interventions are appropriate.

The view taken in this chapter is a somewhat pragmatic one. By and large the Commission should play the referee's role, ensuring that member governments' policies are consistent with the agreed objectives of the Community. However, there will be cases where a transfer of regulatory powers to the EC level may be more efficient and where EC institutions might be the appropriate bodies to initiate policies. What should be emphasised is that the division is probably best determined on a case-by-case basis. For example, in the setting of technical standards and specifications for products it is possible to conceive of situations where EC-wide agreement will yield the best results but there will be others where there is considerable scope for differing national specifications (see below, section 4.3).

The chapter proceeds as follows. Section 2 outlines the form an actively interventionist policy might take and considers why such an approach might not yield the results that are often claimed for it. Section 3 examines the market orientated approach and suggests areas where active EC involvement might be useful. Finally, Section 4 briefly looks at the question of the appropriate division of responsibility between governments and the Commission in relation to three areas – subsidies, competition policy and technical standards.

2.2 INTERVENTIONIST INDUSTRIAL POLICY

A number of authors (eg. Krugman 1987 and Nevin 1990) in their discussions of the integration of the EC economies have emphasised two microeconomic processes through which this integration will be achieved. One is via the effects of comparative advantage and the increasing specialisation of countries within the EC, resulting in an increase in *inter-industry* trade. The other is the benefit that arises from the achievement of economies of scale as firms facing an expanded market increase the size of production units. This effect will be associated with an increase in *intra-industry* trade. Considerable emphasis has been laid on the gain from scale economies, with the EC estimates suggesting that they amount to more than a quarter of the total and possibly up to 35 per cent (Cecchini 1988, p.84, Emerson 1988, p.203). These are derived from cost reductions of between 1 and 6 per cent in about one third of industries in the industry and energy sectors and averaging 1.5 per cent over all industry (Emerson 1988, p.199).

If benefits of this order are attainable, a major question facing the EC is the kind of policy that should be pursued to realise the benefits. There would appear to be two main options for industrial policy; either the EC institutions could take an active role in promoting the restructuring of European industry or a market-based policy could be pursued.

2.2.1 Developmental Intervention

An interventionist policy would set out to encourage the formation of large European businesses and joint ventures to take full advantage of the potential for economies of scale. The use of the term 'developmental' follows that of David Marquand (1988) who wrote of the "developmental State' as one which plays a aiding role in encouraging the growth of domestic industry. It is also known as a policy of picking winners since the authorities play an important part in selecting and supporting sectors and firms which are regarded as essential for the long run growth and prosperity of the economy. Although such a policy is often associated with state ownership as well as direction, as in the case of France, the approach does not necessarily imply any increase in the degree of public ownership. Japan and the role of MITI is one of Marquand's examples.

Apart from the economies of scale gains two other benefits from the interventionist approach can be identified. The first is that the EC could select for special promotion particular sectors that are deemed essential for international competition. The essence of the argument is that Europe's competitive position in relation to Japan and the U.S. would thereby be enhanced. The obvious candidates for special treatment lie in the high technology sector. Second, given that the balance of industrial advantage is continually changing in the world economy, a directly interventionist EC–wide policy could aid the adjustment not only by backing the rising industries but also by easing the contraction of declining sectors such as steel and shipbuilding. This could be taken a stage further by regarding these declining industries as being in a 'developmental' phase of restructuring, and actively promoting their rejuvenation (Jacquemin 1984).

For Europe after *1992* such an approach might mean policies somewhat similar to those recommended in the 1983 French Memorandum on industrial and trade policy (see Pearce and Sutton 1986). Although the Memorandum was specifically concerned with the development of a European high technology sector, its approach can be regarded having a more general application especially in its linking of protectionist trade policies and interventionist industrial policies. In its trade aspects the Memorandum had something of a Fortress Europe flavour, advocating a reduction of intra-EC barriers but matched by a raising of external ones, albeit temporarily. An important industrial policy recommendation was that competition policies should be formulated with reference to the EC market as a whole and not to the domestic market of any individual state. There is some apparent logic to this as the removal of barriers within the EC should provide all EC firms with access to member states' markets. Ultimately this would induce entry into a monopolised market and undermine any position of market power achieved following a merger between two sizeable domestic producers. The long run benefit would be a European market dominated by a few large, highly competitive firms who are able to achieve significant scale economies because they are no longer confined to their own national markets. Moreover, they would be in a position to met the challenge from the largest Japanese and U.S. corporations both in terms of cost and in terms of resources devoted to research and development (R and D).

An example of the French approach is provided by the Thomson–Brandt/Grundig affair of 1982–3 in which a French promoted merger fell foul of the German anti-trust regulators.[1] In the rapidly growing and Japanese dominated video market in the early 1980s the nationalised French consumer electronics group, Thomson-Brandt, faced a choice for entry into the market. Either it could link-up with a Japanese (JVC) led consortium which also included Thorn-EMI and AEG-Telefunken, or proceed to find a European partner. Although there are some indications that the Thomson management was predisposed to the Japanese link, the French Government favoured a European solution and promoted the merger with Grundig. Among a number of complications, the merged company would have accounted for 55 per cent of the West German consumer electronics market and would have had close links with the other major European consumer electronics business, Philips. Philips had a 24.5 per cent stake in Grundig. The case clearly points to two alternative conceptions of industrial policy in the EC; that of the French, who were willing to accept less competition in national, and perhaps EC markets, in return for a larger European owned and controlled business, and that of the Germans for whom the maintenance of competitive pressures in national markets remained important.

In the promotion of European business the Thomson-Brandt/Grundig incident and the French Memorandum also raise the issue of the desirability of co-operation between European firms and external ones, especially Japanese. An aggressively pro-European view is often justified on the grounds that in mergers or joint-ventures with non-European firms the European side of the business could easily slip into the sub-contracting or assembly plant role. Fears are often expressed that the European partners to such agreements, as the junior party, might lose their R and D capacity, causing Europe to fall further behind in the high-tech race. In an attempt to promote a more European-orientated business strategy other policies that could find favour therefore include the more extensive use of EC sponsored link-ups for example in the field of R and D and the adoption of policies that favour European firms such as in setting technical standards or in public procurement.

In short, an EC-level industrial policy of the interventionist type offers the advantages of a strategic trade policy (see Krugman 1987) in which European businesses can gain at the expense of their international rivals. In this way the EC Commission could play a strategic international planning role that is complementary to the planning in a large business; it will be able to "influence not only the mix in the portfolio (of businesses and industries), but also the rate of new business development, the redeployment of human and capital resources to growth sectors, an the withdrawal of those same resources from declining sectors" (Scott 1982).[2]

2.2.2 Some doubts about the interventionist strategy

Serious doubt can be cast on the developmental approach to producing "European Champions" for many reasons, especially if it is accompanied by direct or indirect protection. Not least is the fact that at present the institutional mechanisms do not exist in the EC for promoting specific industries by direct intervention, although it could be argued that the policy would be best pursued by national governments. The powers the Commission does have lie in the restraints that can be placed on state aids, the investigation of uncompetitive practices and the use of protective measures to insulate EC industry from outside competition. An example of this can be seen in the restructuring of the textile industry in the 1970s after the negotiation of the Multi-Fibre Arrangement (see Swann 1983, Ch.6). High technology and steel perhaps provide exceptions. However, the support for high technology covers more than one industrial sector and finances scientific and technological research rather than industrial support. The Community powers over the steel industry are rather greater but they are derived from the ECSC treaty. They include control over imports, the power to lend or withhold finance for investment, and the ability to influence prices and outputs, with price controls and output quotas available in crisis situations.

It is of course not impossible for the Commission to assume greater powers over industrial policy; in the current circumstances, however, it is unlikely to be able to do so. Countries such as Britain and Germany, given their present governments, are unlikely to sanction greater interventionist powers for the Commission especially when their domestic policy has tended towards market liberalism. Moreover, in countries such as France the close links between government and industry have been fostered over many years. Indeed, in France it is generally accepted irrespective of the political complexion of the government, that the state ought to play a leading role in directing industry (see for example Stoffaës 1984).[3] Just as important is that the whole tenor of the *1992* proposals is in keeping with a policy of opening-up the European markets and increasing competition. According to the EC's own estimates, the benefits of increased competition – the reduction of monopoly rents and X-inefficiency – amount to 46 billion ECU or about one quarter of the total gain from the integration programme (Emerson, 1988). Policies that will reduce the level of internal competition within the EC economies are, therefore, unlikely to be widely encouraged or supported.

More specific economic objections can also be put forward. An important one is that the evidence on economies of scale does not indicate that firms need a market of European dimensions to achieve technical economies in many industries. In its assessment, the Commission notes that there are a large number of industries where there are significant technical economies available (see Table 1). Moreover, many of these are in fields that are important for the EC economies' output and employment. However, in a survey of 68 plants in different sectors of industry there were very few in which the minimum efficient scale (MES) exceeded 10 per cent of the Community market – only 11 per cent – and a large majority (73 per cent) in which the MES accounted for 5 per cent or less of the EC market (see Table 2). In other words, the EC market could accommodate in most industries at least 20 plants of minimum efficient scale.

Table 2.1
Economies of scale in a selection of manufacturing industries

Industry	Cost disadvantage at half MES	Comments
Motor vehicles	6–9%	Very substantial EOS[2] in production and in development costs.
Other means of transport	8–20%	Variable EOS: small for cycles and shipbuilding (although economies are possible through series production level), very substantial in aircraft (development costs).
Chemical industry	2,5–15%	Substantial EOS in production processes. In some segments of the industry (pharmaceutical products), R&D is an important source of EOS.
Man-made fibres	5–10%	Substantial EOS in general.
Metals	> 6%	Substantial EOS in general for production processes. Also possible in production and series production.
Office machinery	3–6%	Substantial EOS at product level.
Mechanical engineering	3–10%	Limited EOS at firm level but substantial production.
Electrical engineering	5–15%	Substantial EOS at product level and for development costs.
Instrument engineering	5–15%	Substantial EOS at product level, via development costs.
Paper, printing and publishing	8–36%	Substantial EOS in paper mills and, in particular, printing (books).
Non-metallic mineral products	> 6%	Substantial EOS in cement and flat glass production processes. In other branches, optimum plant size is small compared with the optimum size for the industry.
Metal articles	5–10% (castings)	EOS are lower at plant level but possible at production and series production level.
Rubber and plastics	3–6%	Moderate EOS in tyre manufacture. Small EOS in factories making rubber and moulded plastic articles but potential for EOS at product and series production level.
Drink and tobacco	1–6%	Moderate EOS in breweries. Small EOS in cigarette factories. In marketing, EOS are considerable.
Food	3,5–21%	Principal source of EOS is the individual plant. EOS at marketing and distribution level.

Source: Emerson, 1988

27

Table 2.2

MES as a percentage of the community market in a sample of 68 industries

MES as % of community production total	Distribution of sample[1]
0–1	29
1–2,5	25
2,5–5	19
5–10	16
10–20	7
20–50	3
50–100	1
100 and over	—

[1] Percentage of plants in the sample (68 altogether) falling within each category.

Source: Emerson, 1988

Table 2.3

UK industries in which MES exceeds 20% of the UK market

Industry UK	MES as % of UK product	MES as % of EEC product	Number of firms, 1983
221: iron and steel	72	10	148
223: steel wire	20	4	442
224: aluminium	114	15	591
251: chemicals	23–100	3–50	827
256: fertilizers	23	4	644
321: tractors	98	19	667
326: ball-bearings	20	2	1140
342: electrical equipment	60	6	1228
344: telecommunications equipment	50	10	1603
345: TV sets, etc.	40	9	736
346: domestic appliances	57–85	10–11	234
351: motor vehicles	200	20	187
361: marine engines	30	5	1105
364: aircraft	100 +	?	312
429: tobacco	24	6	19

Source: Emerson, 1988; Geroski, 1989a

Perhaps more important is the significance of scale economies for national markets. As Geroski (1989a) has shown from the U.K. figures, even where the MES is high in relation to the market there is still room for a considerable number of firms. This is illustrated in Table 3. The implication is that the cost disadvantage of operating at less than MES is either reasonably small or compensated for by product quality differences, product differentiation and specialist or niche markets.

The concentration on technical economies ignores other benefits of size: these are economies of scale that arise at firm rather than plant level. These often occur in the areas of marketing and distribution, R and D, finance and product development. In finance for example the Commission cites a finding that large firms have a four per cent interest rate advantage over small firms on borrowed funds (Emerson 1988). On the other hand much of the evidence points to the importance of diseconomies at the firm level due to managerial, organisational and industrial relations problems offsetting the technical economies. Prais (1981) suggests that differences in plant productivity are best explained by factors such as labour relations and investment in training rather than size alone. Geroski and Jacquemin (1985) quote figures that show strike activity rising with plant size almost exponentially. Finally, much has been written on the 'disappointing marriage', to use a well-worn phrase, that many mergers have produced. If many domestic mergers have failed to produce the expected synergy effects there seems little reason to expect any better performance following a European-wide restructuring of companies where management cultures and so on are likely to show even greater differences. Naturally, this does not necessarily mean that there will not be particular cases where success and benefits are great, it is the generality of the effect that is open to question.

One consequence of the restructuring of European industry into larger units will be to reduce the diversity in the range of products available to consumers. Economies of scale, at least on the technical front, normally arise from standardisation and long production runs. However, the standardisation of output, even at lower prices, may raise the welfare of consumers rather less than it would have had a wider range of goods became available. Consider the chocolate market as an example. Consumers may feel better off having a choice of British and Continental chocolate at a slightly higher price, though possibly below the pre–*1992* prices – than one uniform type of chocolate at lower price. In other words consumers prefer and are willing to pay for diversity in the range of goods and, furthermore, the demand for a wide range of products is likely to increase as real incomes rise.

This diversity argument (due to Geroski 1989b and Kay 1989) added to the likelihood that national markets will remain distinctive after *1992* due to factors such as language, tradition, cultural differences etc also casts doubt on the importance of scale economies in many industries. What is more, as Pelkmans and Winters (1988, p.22) have pointed out, developments in computer-aided manufacture and the increasing deployment of flexible management and working systems has reduced the importance of technical economies. Indeed, such developments significantly reduce the cost disadvantage of small and medium-sized production units, and add to the potential for supplying a diverse range of products to a prosperous European market with a wide range of tastes.

The charge that Europe's firms are too small by international standards to compete on international markets can also be dismissed as a general proposition. In chemicals for example four out of the world's top five are European businesses,[4] and in motor vehicles V.W. and Fiat rank as world scale producers. A deliberate policy to encourage the creation of a few large companies in Europe, even operating on a continental scale is also no guarantee that undue market power will not be exercised and competitive forces stifled. This is borne out by the post-war history of the U.S. automobile and steel industries where high concentration and the resulting collusive behaviour can be regarded as the cause of these industries' long run problems (see Gowland and James 1991).

The effect of larger firms and reduced competition would be aggravated by the use of protective barriers to prevent effective competition from outside the EC. As a recent study of the French economy has shown (Adams, 1989), increasing external competition is far more important in accounting for the success of French industry since the war than the industrial and planning policies. In a similar way, an emphasis on EC firm link-ups as opposed to joint ventures or mergers with international businesses, or the granting of preferential treatment in public procurement – both forms of strategic protection – are not on the whole conducive to increasing competitive forces within the EC. It should be added, however, that there may be situations where such action is consistent with greater competition (see below).

2.3 MARKET-BASED INTERVENTION

The alternative to a directly interventionist policy is to opt for a free market approach by taking measures to improve the effectiveness of the workings of the market mechanism. This concentrates on increasing the degree of competition and improving the responsiveness of firms to market signals. The traditional approach of economic theory is to emphasise the structure of an industry and the conduct of firms as the prime determinants of performance. There is, thus, a tendency to lay stress on concentration within an industry and the way in which firms compete, or avoid competing. This explains comments in the Commission's report on *1992* such as:

> "The results (on economies of scale) show that in most industries in question, the Community market can accommodate up to 20 plants of minimum efficient size, whereas the national markets of the four largest economies in the Community could accommodate only four" (Emerson 1988, p.132)

i.e. there is much more scope for competition and much less for collusive behaviour in the integrated Community market.

Recent developments, however, have shifted the focus of the sources of competitive pressure on firms. Geroski and Jacquemin (1985), for example, have argued that the principal factor that determines both static, technological and allocative efficiency on the one hand and dynamic efficiency on the other is the ease with which firms can enter into or exit from an industry. This ties in closely with Baumol's idea of contestable markets (Baumol, 1982). In an industry where there is potential for the exercise of market power new entry or the threat of new entry is important because it will discipline existing firms, reducing the scope for realising monopoly rents and encouraging the elimination of X–inefficiency. As regards dynamic efficiency there are good reasons for thinking, and evidence to support the view that new competition is a most important stimulus to innovation and to their dissemination throughout industry.

Given the importance attached to innovation by the proponents of *1992* it is worth dwelling on this area a little. It seems reasonable to suggest that new firms have less to lose from an innovation and are more likely to innovate than existing firms in an industry (Geroski and Jacquemin, 1985). The reason is that existing firms have to justify new innovations on the basis of the likely *increase* in profits, whereas for the new entrant it is the whole of the profit that is important. New firms also will not be constrained by past investments that are costly to scrap and replace; new plant can be tailor-made to incorporate new processes and to produce new products. Finally, there is the very general point that a protected market position, with ensured monopoly rents destroys any incentive to innovate. In this case it is the lack of competition that is the cause of the unwillingness to innovate, competition that may have come from firms within the industry, or actual and potential new entrants. Once again the U.S. steel industry provides a clear example of the link between the lack of competition and a failure to innovate. In the 1960s and 1970s this highly concentrated industry was noted for its slowness in introducing up-to-date production methods such as continuous casting and the Basic Oxygen Furnace (see Gowland and James, 1991).

According to Geroski and Jacquemin (1985) there are three main ways in which new entry helps to stimulate the introduction of innovations and to diffuse new products and processes throughout an industry:[5]

i) The new entrant introduces an existing but unadopted method or product forcing existing firms to respond by adopting the innovation. The introduction of coin operated dry cleaning in the U.K. in the 1960s is an example.

ii) The new entrant introduces a new product or process forcing the existing firms to adopt it. An example is the use of computer assisted design in U.S. manufacturing. Incumbents such as General Electric responded by taking over the CAD suppliers.

iii) The new entrant's innovation produces a counter-innovation by existing firms. It is also likely that counter-innovations can be provoked by imitative entry. A useful example of a firm which has probably adopted a more innovative strategy than it might have in the absence of both innovative and imitative entry is IBM. In general it has pursued a "fast second" strategy, responding quickly to new innovations with their own version.

The empirical evidence is also supportive of the link between the intensity of competition and the rate of innovation in industry. In a recent study, Geroski (1987)[6] found that, along with the rate of technical progress and the rate of growth of output, both the degree of concentration and the ease of market access were important determinants of innovation.

The market based approach would therefore entail a vigorous anti-trust policy aimed at maintaining competitive pressures throughout the markets of the EC A major thrust of the policy would be to reduce both structural and behavioural (or strategic) barriers to the mobility of firms as these barriers, as well as the structure of an industry and the conduct of firms within it, are critical in affecting economic performance. In some respects the *1992* programme can be regarded as an example of this very policy since it is designed to ease the entry of firms into different and previously separate segments of the EC markets. However, as Geroski and Schwalbach (1989) have shown there are still very significant entry barriers in the European economies in many industries.

The Geroski and Schwalbach study indicates that in U.K. industry entry barriers permit firms to mark-up by about 15 per cent on costs before attracting entry. This is an average figure; the actual barriers vary across industry groups from about 6 per cent to 35 per cent. Similar results were obtained for West German industry. The main cause of the barriers in the U.K. were found to be advertising intensity, and the spurs to entry apart from profit were market size and growth. Capital intensity on the other hand was not significant. In West Germany, however, the critical barrier was economies of scale, and they also included capital intensity and R and D outlay. Of particular relevance to the discussion of *1992* is the finding for the U.K. that the stimulus to foreign entry given by high profits was considerably less than the response of domestic firms – about one fifth as much. This suggests that the removal of *1992* type barriers will increase the responsiveness of EC competitors. However, Geroski and Schwalbach also found that on average the height of barriers facing foreign firms was broadly the same as those facing domestic entrants. Thus, while it cannot be dismissed that business behaviour towards entry into other EC markets will change – this is one of the main objectives of the intensive marketing of *1992* – it does suggest that the barriers *1992* seeks to remove are not the only or perhaps the main type of entry barrier.

The implication of the Geroski and Schwalbach study is that the *1992* measures in themselves may have little effect on real barriers to entry in national markets and that we should not expect too much in terms of increased industrial efficiency. The lesson for competition policy is that it might suggest entry barriers are best attacked by national regulators, particularly if the nature of the barriers differs between countries and across industries. But as discussed in section 4, there could be good reason for a greater role for the Commission in this area as well.

On the whole economists tend to be in agreement on the beneficial effects of competition on economic efficiency in industry. However, it is also accepted that there are situations where intervention is necessary. If a market-based policy is to be pursued the interventions that can be justified are not of the market replacing type, as is the case with the developmental approach, but should be market improving. Competition policy is one form, but it is essentially negative; some market failures may require a more activist approach. In general there seem to be four reasons for interventions of this type:

a) *Externalities*
It can be argued that there are substantial external benefits in the setting of common technical standards as these will promote greater specialisation and competition in EC industry. The high technology and communications industries have often been cited as examples; thus, a telephone system becomes more valuable to subscribers the more subscribers there are. The benefits can also be illustrated by the competitive developments in the computing industry stimulated by IBM's change to a strategy of plug-compatibles in the 1970s. Not only did peripherals producers compete with IBM and each other but they were also able to specialise in different parts of the computer system, driving down costs and raising product quality (see Gowland and James, 1991). A current European example is the cellular 'phone market (see Geroski 1989a).

b) *Economies of scale*
Basic research in high technology industries requires substantial sunk costs, but if national markets are too small for these to be recovered R and D expenditure may be sub-optimal. This is the justification for joint EC-private sector initiatives such as ESPRIT which seeks to promote link-ups between EC based firms in the information technology

34

industries. Of course the widening of the European market after *1992* somewhat reduces the force of this argument. However, such projects could also generate external benefits: if the results of 'basic' research can be shared and common standards established for product development economic efficiency may be improved as long as care is taken to ensure that inter-firm agreements do not spread from 'basic' research to other areas of business.

c) *Strategic entry into international markets*
Some markets may be of such a scale, and dominated by a large non-European business that domestic firms are unable to enter the industry. European-wide joint ventures promoted by the EC may provide an answer to this as it has in the case of the Airbus challenge to the U.S.'s dominant position in the civil aircraft industry. However, here one must be clear about the intentions of the joint venture (or merger); ie. whether it is a true strategic entry into a monopolised market or simply a means of supporting an ailing domestic industry. There are unlikely to be many cases like Airbus and care must be taken to ensure that competition is genuine and benefits consumers. The liberalisation of public procurement, giving freedom of choice over supplier to public agencies and nationalised industries will be an important complementary step (see Hartley, in this volume, Chapter 6).

d) *Overcoming strategic exit barriers*
In a declining industry there may be strategic reasons why firms do not exit. The payoff to those leaving may be less that for those remaining and this will deter any one firm from exiting first. The result will be a moribund industry with low rates of return, low investment and a poor record on innovation. Steel has been quoted as an example here (Geroski and Jacquemin, 1985). The success of the Davignon Plan of the late 1970s and early 1980s has been upheld as an illustration of the way in which co-ordinated restructuring of an industry can take place (see Geroski and Jacquemin, 1985 and Swann 1983), although there were costs in the form of the imposition of price controls, production quotas and import restrictions. Moreover, the plan's success in decreasing European steel capacity can be questioned on the grounds that capacity reduction was achieved because some countries pursued a more vigorous market orientated policy than others. Britain and Italy can be contrasted in this respect.

35

Any one of these situations may well provide justifiable reasons for direct intervention in particular cases but they are not likely to be applicable to industry as a whole. The promotion of competition within the EC is likely to be the most effective adjunct to the market access and competition enhancing effects of the *1992* measures.

2.4 CENTRALISED OR DECENTRALISED POLICY MAKING

The advocacy of a market orientated policy after *1992* leaves open the question of the proper division of functions between the EC Commission and national governments. It is an issue that is common to all areas of policy making including the industrial. There are in fact two related issues here; the first is the extent to which policy making should be transferred to the EC level or remain with national governments; the second is whether policy implementation should be through EC institutions or national ones. One approach which has recently received support is to apply the principle of 'subsidiarity' (see Helm and Smith, 1989 and Curzon-Price, 1989). This suggests that powers should be devolved to the most local level possible unless there are significant benefits from a more centralised policy. The reasons for preferring devolved decision making and implementation are associated with the familiar problems of bureaucracies: information is more costly to acquire and so is implementation; local policies can reflect local preferences more accurately; and local policies can be adapted to meet local market conditions.

Where there are external effects of policies that spill over beyond the national market there may be a good case for a centrally determined policy ie. at the EC level, although the implementation does not necessarily need to be centralised. Some forms of pollution control are classic examples, for example, acid rain. In terms of industrial policy there are a number of areas where the Commission's role could be considered important, three of which are considered briefly below.

2.4.1 Subsidies (State Aids)

The extent to which national governments subsidise their industries can be gleaned from the details given in Tables 4, 5 and 6. Taken from the

EC's "First Survey of State Aids in the EC" (EC 1989), they show that on average subsidies amount to some 3 per cent of EC GNP and, by and large, most of this comes from national governments. Of the EC funds, about 20 per cent of the total, approximately 80 per cent went to agriculture. Support to industry therefore makes up the lion's share of the total support given by governments, between 5 and 6 per cent of manufacturing value added (Table 5). The degree of support, however, varies considerably between countries, ranging at the top end from around 16 per cent in Italy down to 2–3 per cent in Denmark, West Germany and the U.K. There is also considerable variation in the destination of the aid and the types of aid instruments used – grants, tax allowances, equity stakes and the like. Table 6 compares the aid given in four countries distinguishing between general aid that is available to all sectors (under the heading horizontal objectives) from support to specific sectors. It is the latter that is considered to be the most distortionary.

State aids constitute an obvious area for EC-wide regulation, a concern which should be heightened by the extensive use of support in many EC economies. Faced with increasing competition as a result of *1992* it is conceivable that national governments might seek to obtain a competitive advantage for their domestic industries through the use of grants, soft loans, tax advantages and other forms of state support. Not only would this distort competition and reduce economic efficiency, thereby negating some of the beneficial effects of removing trade barriers, it also puts firms in countries with non-interventionist governments at a disadvantage. This is the familiar "level playing field" argument. A further objection to giving governments too much lattitude in their industrial support policies is that a competitive approach to industrial policy may develop, with each country trying to give its own firms advantages in the wider EC markets. The competitive use of strategic industrial policies would in the end raise the level of subsidies in the Community, further misallocating resources and producing possibly undesirable redistribution effects.

In recognition of some of the potential ill-effects of state aids the EC Commission's policy has developed rapidly over the past few years (see the Seventeenth and Eighteenth Reports on Competition Policy, EC 1988 and 1989). There has been increasing stringency in the enforcement of EC regulations along with a rising number of notifications of aid schemes, from 124 in 1986 to 375 in 1988. In addition the Commission is

37

Table 2.4
State aids in the E.C. (1981–86 annual average)

	National state aid (bn ECU)	*E.C. aid (bn ECU)*	*Total aid as a % of GND*
Belgium	4.0	0.8	4.1
Denmark	0.8	0.8	1.3
Germany	19.1	3.5	2.5
Greece	1.0	1.3	2.5
France	16.7	4.6	2.7
Ireland	1.1	1.2	5.3
Italy	27.7	4.1	5.7
Luxembourg	0.2	0	6
Netherlands	2.2	1.9	1.5
U.K.	9.4	2.7	1.8
EEC10	82.3	22.0	3.0

Source: European Commission, 1989

Table 2.5
State aids to manufacturing in the E.C. (1981–86 annual average)

	Total aid as a % of gross value added	*Total aid as a % of gross value added excluding steel and shipbuilding*	*Total aid per employee (ECU)*
Belgium	6.4	4.5	1113
Denmark	2.8	1.7	353
Germany	3.0	2.9	761
Greece	12.9	13.9	278
France	4.9	3.6	792
Ireland	12.9	12.3	1036
Italy	16.7	15.8	1357
Luxembourg	7.3	3.5	1562
Netherlands	4.1	4.1	444
U.K.	3.8	2.9	396
EEC10	6.2	5.5	771

Source: European Commission, 1989

keen to introduce a new scheme for the notification and monitoring of aids that improves the information available. In 1988 the proposals were applied to the motor vehicle sector: from January 1st member states were required to notify the Commission of all aid to motor vehicle manufacturers for projects exceeding 12m ECU and to prepare annual reports on all aid payments to the sector (Eighteenth Report, EC 1988, pp.145–6).

Perhaps the EC policy is best illustrated by reference to two recent cases, those of Renault and the British Aerospace purchase of the Rover Group. In both cases uppermost in the Commission's mind seems to have been the possibility that the subsidies paid to the firms would give them a competitive advantage over their European rivals who were not in receipt of such support.

Table 2.6
State aid in four E.C. countries (1981–86 annual averages, MECU)
(% of total in brackets)

	France	Germany	Italy	U.K.
1. Agriculture and Fisheries	2914.9 (17)	1419.5 (7)	1951.4 (7)	1157.0 (12)
2. Horizontal objectives	3394.9 (20)	2474.7 (13)	8943.2 (32)	1587.8 (17)
– Innovation and R and D	220.5	1383.8	732.6	542.8
– Trade/Export	2091.2	99	1328.1	748.8
– General Investment	921.0	98.2	1234.1	138.5
– Others	162.0	893.7	5648.4	157.8
3. Sectors in industry	9993.9 (60)	11771.7 (62)	10956.4 (40)	5311.4 (56)
– Steel	1513.2	370.5	1629.2	703.2
– Shipbuilding	507.1	176.2	236.7	483.5
– Transport	4407.9	5930.8	8845.9	1522.2
– Coal	2285.3	5002.6	—	2068.9
– Other crisis sectors	616.2	0	934.4	408.6
– Growth sectors	318.4	156.8	416.4	41.7
– Others	345.4	134.9	1245.4	23.6
4. Regional aid	383.4 (2)	3447.4 (18)	5855.2 (21)	1372.3 (15)
5. Total	16,687.1	19113.1	27706.2	9,428.6

Source: E.C. Commission 1989

In the Renault case the Commission opened Article 93(2)[7] procedures against the payment of assistance by the French Government to the troubled nationalised French motor company. These included injections by the Government of new equity of FF2 billion in 1986 and again in 1987, and a proposal to repay for Renault long term debt of FF12 billion to a publicly owned bank (Seventeenth Report, EC 1988, pp.167–8). The aid was designed to help change Renault's status from a "régie" – a company with special status and hence an effective state guarantee of survival – to a legal entity subject to normal company law. The ensuing dispute between the Commission and the French Government revolved mainly around the conditions the Commission attached to the aid package, principally that it should use the funds to restructure the company, reducing productive capacity by 25 per cent, as well as changing its legal status. Although the final outcome was something of a compromise, a final settlement in May 1990 resulted in Renault agreeing to repay FF3.5 billion of debt and reinstating FF2.5 billion of long-term debt on its balance sheet (The Economist, 20 May 1990).

In the British Aerospace buyout of Rover the main charge was that in addition to selling the Company at well below its market value (£150 million rather than an estimated £500–600 million), the U.K. Government paid BAe £44 million of so-called 'sweeteners'. These consisted of a subsidy for buying out Rover's existing private shareholders and a delay in paying for the company worth £22 million in savings on interest payments. In a recent ruling the Commission's Competition Commissioner has ordered the company to repay the £44 million 'sweeteners'; this follows previous Commission action in 1988 that reduced a Government cash injection into Rover to wipe out debts from the originally proposed £800 million to £572 million (The Economist, 23 June 1990).

2.4.2 Competition Policy

While state aids have become an increasingly important part of the Community's Competition policy, much of the activity in the past has concerned the more conventional anti-trust type policy, and there is no reason to believe that this will become any less important. It is likely to become more so. The basis of the EC's competition policy is contained in Articles 85 and 86 of the Treaty of Rome, the former dealing with cartels and other restrictive agreements and the latter with the abuse of dominant market positions. They are applied in cases where anti-competitive practices affect trade between member states. Although there is no specific recognition of a merger policy in the Treaty, a ruling in the Continental Can case in the 1970s extended the application of Article 86 to include the establishment of dominant market positions via merger (see Swann, 1983, p.119). Mergers may also be scrutinised under Article 85 since a shareholding in a competitor may be regarded as a restrictive agreement, as in the Philip Morris acquisition of a 25 per cent stake in Rothmans in the early 1980s (see Hay and Vickers 1988). In view of the increasing number and importance of cross-country mergers within the EC – the Commission reports a rise in EC industrial mergers among the top 1,000 European companies from 29 in 1983/4 to 111 in 1987/8 – merger activity seems to be an appropriate area for an extension and clarification of EC policy. Currently there are proposals by the Commission for a directive that would extend its regulatory powers to cover all European scale mergers but as yet (Summer 1990) no agreement has been reached.

Despite the fact that most EC states have their own well-established competition policy, there may well be a good case for extending the scope of EC competition policy or at least bringing national policy into line.[8] As has been noted above, it is unlikely that the *1992* measures will remove all entry barriers: it is conceivable that many national markets will remain protected from new entry, especially oligopolistic ones, by natural barriers or strategic ones erected by domestic businesses. A switch to a more pro-competitive EC policy may provide the surest means of opening up these markets. Also, and perhaps just as important, are the limitations that such a change will place on governments, preventing them from conniving with domestic firms in order to maintain the dominance of home producers. An example of the beneficial impact of EC regulation is provided by the recent British Airways takeover of British Caledonian Airways in which the Commission insisted on far stricter conditions than the U.K.'s MMC before it would allow the merger to proceed.

There are other benefits of an EC level policy.[9] First, it is likely that EC institutions will be less susceptible to regulatory capture than national agencies because they are independent of the interest of any one member state and are therefore more likely to impose stricter conditions or stiffer penalties on firms breeching the competition regulations. National regulatory authorities might be more wary of adversely affecting a domestic producer. Second, the increased likelihood of more strictly administered EC rules may have a deterrent effect and increase firms' compliance. A third beneficial effect could be that the introduction of a common EC competition policy provides an ideal opportunity for countries to improve their system of regulation without having to undertake difficult and time consuming reforms.

However, the argument for a commonly applied policy is open to question. It could be argued that Articles 85 and 86 already cover cases that affect the free flow of trade between member countries, and situations where trade is not affected would seem to be an ideal for the application of the subsidiarity principle, that is, leaving the policy to local regulators. Furthermore, as integration proceeds and inter-county trade increases more cases will automatically come within the jurisdiction of the Commission. Nevertheless, even if the case against wider Community powers is not accepted there are good reasons for bringing domestic policy into line with EC policy since inconsistencies can be costly for the regulators and the firms. This has already begun to occur in the U.K. in the field of restrictive agreements (see Hay and Vickers, 1988).

2.4.3 Technical standards

The EC wide harmonization of product specifications and technical standards pose particular difficulties. Insisting on common standards may have the unfortunate effect of "locking-in" Europe to inappropriate technical specifications given developments in international markets. Moreover, they reduce the opportunity for diversity and may adversely affect the incentive to innovate. On the other hand, the alternative approach of competitive standards can mean that domestic producers capture local or national markets and consequently can exercise monopoly power. In addition there is reduced scope for Europe-wide specialisation and the realisation of economies of scale. There is also the risk that national governments may use the setting of competitively lower standards than their rivals to secure a greater proportion of European industry. For a discussion of competition in laxity see Chapter 3.

The current approach of the EC is that of the mutual recognition of different countries' standards given an acceptance of EC-wide minimum

42

standards for safety and consumer protection. This appears to be the correct approach for the broad mass of goods where, with greater information provided to consumers, people are free to make informed choices. Where there are significant and proven scale economies or external effects a common standards may be required (see Van de Gevel and Mayes, 1989).

Finally, two areas where common European standards may prove useful are in the fields of accounting and company law. In combination with a strongly pro-competitive policy, the removal of artificial impediments to the creation of European businesses would provide a firmer basis for the growth of European industry whether it is by internal growth or acquisition. Indeed the growth of firms under such circumstances is more likely to be economically justifiable than an interventionist strategy that artificially encourages mergers and industrial restructuring.

2.5 SUMMARY AND CONCLUSION

It has been maintained in this chapter that the *1992* programme will prove to be most beneficial when accompanied by an industrial policy that encourages competition and improves the operation of market forces. Direct intervention either at the EC level to promote 'European Champions' or at the national level may be counter-productive in many cases. In the latter case competitive national industrial policies will be especially harmful. If a policy environment that is conducive to competition is to be maintained then in many areas, the appropriate role for the Commission and for EC-wide policy is to ensure that national governments do not abuse their position for the competitive advantage of domestic industries. This is most apparent in industrial support policies. In other words EC industrial policy after *1992* is not just about regulating firms but also about regulating governments.

NOTES

1. Pearce and Sutton (1986) discuss this case at some length.
2. Quoted in Jacquemin (1984). See also note 13 in Jacquemin (1984, Introduction).

3. Hayward (1986), however, questions the extent to which the French Government has been able to influence industry. In his view it is the industrialists who have had the upper hand (see Chapter 12).
4. The top five are Duport, BASF, Bayer Hoechst and ICI.
5. The examples quoted are all taken from Geroski and Jacquemin (1985).
6. The study is summarised in Emerson (1988).
7. See Swann (1983, pp.45–58) for a discussion of state aids and the Articles of the Treaty of Rome.
8. As Kay and Posner (1989) note, although not all EC countries have the well established anti-trust institutions of the U.K. or West Germany and government influence is exerted more informally, it is not necessarily less powerful.
9. The arguments are reviewed in Gatsois and Seabright (1989).

REFERENCES

Adams, W.J. (1989) *The Restructuring of the French Economy: Government and the rise of Market Competition since World War II*, Brookings, Washington.

Baumol, W.J. (1982) "Contestable Markets', *American Economic Review.*

Curzon-Price, V. (1989) 'Three Models of European Integration', in R. Dahrendorf *et al Whose Europe?*, I.E.A., London.

Davis, E. et al (1989) *1992: Myths and Realtieis,* Centre for Business Strategy, London Business School.

E.C. (1988) *Seventeenth Report on Competition Policy* (1987), Commission for the E.C.

E.C. (1989) *Eighteenth Report on Competition Policy* (1988), Commission for the E.C.

E.C. (1989b) *First Survey on State Aids in the European Community,* Commission for the E.C.

Emerson, M. et al (1988), *The Economics of 1992,* O.U.P., Oxford.

Gatsios, K. and P. Seabright (1989) 'Regulation in the European Community', *Oxford Review of Economic Policy,* Vol.5, No.2, Summer 1989.

Geroski, P.A. (1987) *Competition and Innovation,* E.C. Commission, Brussels.

Geroski, P.A. (1989a) 'European Industrial Policy and Industrial Policy in Europe', *Oxford Review of Economic Policy,* Summer 1989, Vol.5, No.2.

Geroski, P.A. (1989b) 'The Choice between diversity and scale' in E. Davis et al (1989).

Geroski, P.A. and A. Jacquemin (1985) 'Industrial change, barriers in mobility and European Industrial Policy', *Economic Policy* 1.

Geroski, P.A. and J. Schwalbach *Barriers to Entry and Intensity of Competition in European Markets,* E.C. Commission.

Gowland, D.H. and James, S. (1991), 'Manufacturing' in G. Hodgson (ed.) *The United Satates: A Handbook,* Facts on File Inc., New York, forthcoming.

Hay, D. and J. Vickers (1988) 'The Reform of U.K. Competition Policy', *National Institute Economic Review,* No.125, August 1988.

Hayward, J. (1986) *The State and the Market Economy,* Wheatsheaf, Brighton.

Helm, D. and S. Smith (1989) 'Economic Integration and the Role of the State', *Oxford Review of Economic Policy,* Vol.5, No.2, Summar 1989.

Jacquemin, A. (ed) (1984) *European Industry: Public Policy and Corporate Strategy Oxford University Press,* Oxford.

Jacquemin, A. and A. Sapir (eds) (1990) *The European Intetnal Market: Trade and Competition Oxford University Press,* Oxford.

Krugman, P.R. (1987) 'Economic Integration in Europe: Some conceptual issues' in T. Padoa-Schioppa (1987), reprinted in Jacquemin and Sapir (1990).

Marquard, D. (1988) *The Unprincipled Society,* Jonathan Cape, London.

Neven, D.J. (1990) 'Gains and Losses from 1992', *Economic Policy,* April 1990, Vol.5, No.1.

Padoa-Schioppa, T. et al (1987) *Efficiency, Stability and Equity: A Strategy for the Evolution of the Economic System of the E.C.,* Oxford University Press, Oxford.

Pearce, J. and J. Sutton (1986) *Protection and Industrial Policy in Europe,* R11A/ Routledge, London.

Pelkmans, J. and A. Winters *Europe's Domestic Market,* Chatham House Papers No.43, R11A/Routledge, London.

Prais, S. (1981) *Productivity and Industrial Structure,* Cambridge University Press, Cambridge.

Scott, B.B. (1982) 'Can Industry Survive the Welfare State', *Harvard Business Review,* Sept/Oct 1982.

Stoffaës, C. (1984) in Jacquemin (1984).

Swann, D. (1983) *Competition and Industrial Policy in the European Community,* Methuen, London.

Van De Gavel, A. and D.G. Mayes (1989) '1992: Removing the Barriers', *National Institute Economic Review,* No.129, August 1989.

3 Financial policy after 1992

D.H. Gowland

3.1 INTRODUCTION

Financial policy has both a macroeconomic and a microeconomic dimension. Its *macroeconomic aspect* comprises attempts to influence inflation and unemployment by means of monetary, exchange rate, credit and interest rate policy. Although much less publicised, the *microeconomic aspect* of financial policy is both more important and has usually been more central to policy makers. The microeconomic objectives of financial policy are the efficiency and stability of the financial system. The dangers of mistakes in this field are revealed by the $500 billion cost to the US Treasury of the Savings and Loans fiasco, below. The instruments used to achieve this are a plethora of regulatory devices, such as deposit insurance, reinforced by direct intervention by national governments, usually in the form of a central bank or a specialist agency such as the SEC (Securities and Exchange Commission) in the USA, SIB (Securities and Investments Board) in the UK and CONSOB in Italy. Thus it includes, for example, investor protection and policies designed to avert bank failures. Microeconomic financial policy often seeks to provide improved services for the rest of the economy, for example, cheaper or more readily available loan finance. In recent years the creation of jobs, in financial services, has become a major goal of financial policy, especially in the UK and France.

In this chapter I will examine the impact of *1992* on the conduct of both macro and micro financial policy. Indeed the two are inextricably linked. Failure to appreciate this has frequently been an error of, especially UK, government policy in its failure to understand the relationship between membership of the exchange rate mechanism (ERM) of the European Monetary System (EMS) and achievement of its microeconomic objectives – a "level playing field" that would permit free and fair competition in financial services through the European Community (Gowland, 1988). Moreover microeconomic actions frequently constrain macroeconomic policy. In particular commitments to fair competition in finance combined with the abolition of exchange control restrict the use of most traditional instruments of macroeconomic policy. These include not only direct controls but, I argue below, budgetary policy. It is the purpose of this chapter to delimit the implications of *1992* for conduct of financial policy in the member states of the European Community over the next decade or so, that is in what is intended to be the transition period leading up to the attainment of both political and economic and monetary union. I am concentrating upon this not only because it is the more immediate but because the nature and indeed the very feasibility of any longer-term goals depend upon what happens in the immediate future.

1992 is a convenient shorthand to describe a variety of policy initiatives agreed by the European Community. Besides the commitment to the internal market itself the most important is the European Monetary System and in particular its exchange rate mechanism (ERM), a system of pegging exchange rates within narrow bands with, however, adjustable parities.[1] The EMS also includes a partial pooling of reserves in the European Cooperation Fund and a system of central bank coordination through regular meetings of their Governors. Attempts to promote a wider use of the ECU (European Currency Unit)[2] are one of the charges of the central bank governors. However, there are disagreements about whether a market-oriented approach is preferable to a more dirigiste approach. The Bank of England and Bundesbank both argue for the former while the European Commission and most of the remaining members of the European Community prefer the latter as embodied in the Delors report (1989).

Any market-oriented approach to economic integration necessarily involves *the abolition of all exchange control:* a point frequently made by the UK after it abandoned exchange control in October 1979. Finally in response to British pressure the EC accepted this at Hanover in June 1988, with waivers for Italy (until 1992) and Greece, Spain and Portugal until, at the earliest, 1995. The commitment became more central after the Madrid Summit in 1989. In consequence in the course of the first half of 1990 Italy and France abandoned their remaining formal exchange control devices.

The EC has promulgated a number of directives concerning finance, especially in banking but also covering stock exchange practice, insurance and fund management services. Crucially these embody the principle of *country of origin regulation* as opposed to *host country regulations* (Gowland, 1988; Llewellyn, 1988; see chapter 4 for the parallel discussion of tax policy). With host country regulation, a bank would be permitted to operate in any member state of the EC so long as but only so long as it obeyed the regulations of the country in which it operated. Hence, for example, a British bank could operate in, say, Italy so long as but only so long as it operated under Italian regulatory code. (Throughout this section the example of a bank is used but the same arguments apply with equal force to all financial institutions.) With country of origin regulation, a bank can in effect choose which regulatory code it wishes to obey. A UK bank could set up an Italian subsidiary and operate under Italian rules in Italy. Alternatively it could choose to operate under UK rules in Italy. Still more choices are available. A subsidiary could be registered in Portugal (or any other member of the EC) with the intention of operating as a bank in Italy. Hence a bank wishing to establish itself in Italy can choose from amongst 12 sets of rules and operate accordingly; the four cases it can also operate under EC rules. The opportunity to choose one's regulator is not unique to the European Community, see the discussion in Gowland (1990) pp. 32–4. It is often the case in the USA, where financial firms can choose between federal and state regulation and indeed can often shop around amongst the 50 states. Within the UK, the new regulatory system introduced in 1986–9 offers many financial institutions the opportunity to choose their regulator. Nevertheless there are dangers inherent in such a choice. The institution is likely to choose the regulatory code it prefers, normally the one which offers it most freedom. Hence country of origin regulation is likely to evolve towards the most liberal already extant among the 12 EC members, or rather towards a *mélange* compromising the most liberal elements of the existing codes. A bank is likely to set up different subsidiaries for different purposes in whichever is the most convenient régime rather as many Texas banks have North Dakota subsidiaries to supply credit cards but Delaware investment management subsidiaries, both operating in Texas. Hence the operative laws in Texas are that mixture of Texan, Delaware and North Decotan rules chosen by the banks.

This tendency will be reinforced by *competition in laxity*. The choice of a particular regulatory régime by a bank etc confers considerable benefits upon both the regulatory agency and the country in which it is sited. The regulatory agency is likely to gain prestige and income as well as a *raison d'être*. If nearly all banks operated in Italy under British or German charters the *Banca d'Italia* would undoubtedly feel a loss of *amour propre* as well as a sense of futility. Contrawise, the Bank of England might well feel a sense of mission and pride. Financial institutions usually pay licence fees to their regulators so the income of the chosen regulator would rise. More importantly there would be considerable employment and pecuniary gains to the country whose regulatory régime was chosen. The incorporation of, say, a Portuguese subsidiary by a German bank to exploit its liberal laws in, say, Belgium would bring business to Lisbon lawyers, accountants, etc. Moreover, the new subsidiary would usually but not inevitably (Gowland, 1990a) set up its "back office" in Lisbon to carry out the clerical and computer processing of its operations. Such employment gains could be large – as in the case of North Dakota or Delaware. Hence regulators would actively seek to attract banks, etc. to their régimes to obtain these benefits. To do so they would offer the banks a more favourable and more liberal regulatory régime: competition in laxity. Such policy is the centrepiece of the present UK government's employment policy, as outlined in for example the 1990 Budget. Some authors welcome such competition amongst regulators – notably the author in Barro (1988) and King (1989). They argue that competition is likely to lead to a regulatory code that provides both financial institutions and their customers with the features they find useful. Others argue that market failure is too great for this market to work efficiently: notably Llewellyn in for example (1990).

Certainly the decision to opt for country of origin regulation is likely to lead to an extremely permissive and liberal régime wherein financial institutions can do virtually what they please (Gowland, 1988; Llewellyn,

1988). It is therefore instructive to consider why the European Commission has not opted for host country regulation. It is consistent with its preference for country of origin (not destination) in the tax field, see Dosser (1972), Shoup (1967) and the chapter by Jones in this volume. However the Commission has shown that it can regard inconsistency as the hobgoblin of petty minds and by itself this would not have persuaded the Commission unless there were other reasons to reject host country regulation. More significantly the European Commission seems to have accepted that finance is a *contestable* industry in Baumol's (1982) sense – see Gowland (1990a). A contestable industry is one in which both entry *and exit* are relatively costless in the absence of regulatory inhibitions to either. Imagine that profits are high and price exceeds marginal cost in a sector of finance – perhaps loans to small firms in Italy or to consumers in the UK. A German bank would be tempted to enter the market, as in orthodox theory. It would examine the barriers to entry and in their absence would enter according to orthodox theory. Baumol argues that they will further calculate the effect of their entry on profits in the industry: to eliminate the excess profit that attracted them in the first place. At this stage they would wish to leave, hence the crucial relevance of exit costs. If hit and run raiders can enter *and leave* markets costlessly then they will do so whenever price exceeds marginal cost. This will drive price down to marginal cost, hence price will always be equal to marginal cost. Country of origin regulation ensures that regulation can not inhibit contestability: competition in laxity will ensure that someone's rules facilitate exit. On the other hand central banks tend to block at least exit in the name of *integrity of markets* – see the discussion in Gowland (1990) pp. 28, 58. Hence if finance were naturally contestable probably only the Commission approach could render it so in practice. A number of authors have argued that finance is inherently contestable, for example Davies and Davies (1984). The basic argument is that exit costs only exist if there is specific capital and hence sunk costs in the absence of a second-hand market in capital goods. Capital in finance is normally very general, either money or property, although computer systems are likely to be very specific. Whatever the truth of the proposition, which is challenged in the credit rationing literature (Cosci, 1991), the European Commission's policy is postulated upon contestability in finance. Moreover the Commission has reason to feel that member states might not accept the virtues of competition in finance and might prefer a protected market without entry. The *Banca d' Italia* has not licensed a new bank since 1966 (Welsh, 1981).

Thus host country regulation might not lead to an increase in competition, fair or otherwise. Even more important, host country regulation can be used to generate *non-tariff barriers to trade*. An apparently neutral regulation ostensibly designed to promote beneficent ends can be a barrier to trade by accident or design. Until recently Germany had very strict regulations concerning beer which in effect denote all British beer as a danger to health. These have been held to be a non-tariff barrier to trade by denying British breweries a chance to export to Germany even though they could in theory sell in Germany if they were to meet German regulations. Another current case involves Danish attempts to bar the sale of lager in cans on ecological grounds. Is this an innocent, laudable attempt to promote environmental ends or a device designed to protect Carlsberg which concentrates on glass containers and happens to be based in Denmark? The European Commission understandably wishes to avoid opening another such Pandora's Box in finance. Given the different institutional patterns that have emerged in different countries, non-tariff barriers would be especially easy to construct in finance. For instance, a decision to insist that commercial and investment banking be separate could discriminate against German banks. Yet it could be regarded as a legitimate goal of regulation as it has been embodied in both the Japanese (Section 64) and US regulatory codes (Glass-Steagall and SEC Act, Section 144). By adopting country of origin regulations the European Commission has cut the gordian knot to avoid the host of cases which would clog the European Court as it sought to separate reasonable expressions of national preference from unreasonable barriers to fair competition.

Finally, country of origin regulation will act as a powerful incentive to the member states of the EC to adopt unified, harmonized regulations. Regulation can be effective if and only if all 12 member states adopt it, otherwise evasion is possible as described above. In the area of finance the 3rd banking directive is a good example of this although it was also designed to incorporate the G10 banking accord which in its turn superseded the Anglo-American Banking pact (Gowland, 1990, pp. 84–5). This imposes *uniform capital adequacy ratios on banks*. A bank has three sources of funds: equity capital, deposits and non-deposit loan capital of various sorts such as bonds. These are then invested in both

51

fixed assets and various types of loan and investment. Hence a bank's balance sheet might appear as follows

Assets:	Loans	100
	Fixed Assets and other non-loan assets	25
		125

represented by

Liabilities:	deposits	90
	bonds	15
	equity	20

A capital adequacy ratio insists that equity (and sometimes bonds) be at least a specified percentage of total assets. The purpose is to increase the security of depositors' funds. In the above example assets could decline in value to 90 and depositors' funds would still be safe as they have a claim on the assets which takes precedence over bond holders' and equity interests. The greater are bonds and equity the more the bank's assets can decline in value and still be sufficient to repay depositors.

The regulations impose a common ratio on all banks in the European Community and avoid the dangers of competition in laxity by regulators lowering the ratio. However, a number of problems arise with such a regulation, all of which have been tackled by both G10 and the EC.

(a) Definition of assets. In the above example if the bank were allowed to write its fixed assets up to 40 from 25 then the value of its equity would also rise by 15 and so capital adequacy would rise from 29 per cent (35/125) to 35 per cent (50/140). This means that a common set of valuation rules must be laid down otherwise competition in laxity would allow banks to meet a ratio by writing up the value of their assets as for example Nat West did in the UK in 1988. Particular problems arise with property, profits on share holdings (especially in the case of Japanese banks) and valuation of dubious loans, for example to the Third World. If a bank fails to write off bad debts this also artificially boosts its assets.

(b) Some loan capital is a permanent investment in the business like equity but some has to be repaid in the near future and cannot really be regarded as a protection to depositors. In the above example, if the bonds had to be repaid the capital adequacy ratio would fall to 18 per cent (20/110). To deal with this various capital adequacy ratios have to be observed, each to satisfy a different definition of 'capital'.

(c) Different banks' portfolios of loan embody different risks so a uniform ratio is both unfair and inefficient.

(d) A capital adequacy ratio may encourage banks to hold more risky loans, see the survey in Di Cagno (1990). The basic idea is simple: a capital adequacy ratio reduces a bank's profits so it may seek to counteract this by holding riskier but more profitable assets.

This solution to both (c) and (d) adopted by the European regulators (like G10 and the Anglo-American banking pact) is the *risk-weighted capital adequacy ratio*. An immediate and obvious improvement on the simple capital adequacy ratio is that the optimal capital adequacy ratio should depend on the riskiness of the assets. If 5 per cent (however measured) is adequate for bank A with assets of riskiness 80 (however that is measured), it is not adequate for bank B with assets of riskiness 200.

This proposition is undeniable and the Bank of England pioneered the development of such risk-weighted (or adjusted) ratios. They were incorporated into the Anglo-American banking pact of 1986 and the G10 pact of December 1987. Unfortunately, what seemed to the Bank to be the only practicable method of doing this, is controversial.

The Bank's method is to divide a bank's assets into categories. Each category is viewed as having a different risk and so a different capital adequacy ratio is assigned; for example, asset A might be riskless and have a zero requirement, B might be riskier and have a 10 per cent requirement, and so on. Hence a bank's overall capital adequacy requirement is a weighted average of the requirements of the various types of assets it holds. This approach is illustrated hypothetically in the following table.

A conventional capital adequacy ratio would be calculated as a proportion of total assets (500) and a risk-weighted one as a proportion of the risk-adjusted column, 550. Hence, if the requirement were 10 per cent, the requirement would be 55. If the bank were to switch 100 from loans to small companies to large companies, a conventional capital adequacy ratio would be unaffected. This hypothetical risk-weighted one would be reduced by 10 – that is 10 per cent of the new final column, which would then sum to 450; 0.75 (75) + 1 (300) + 2 (50).

Asset	Amount	Risk weight	Adjusted amount
Cash	50	0	0
Government securities	100	0.75	75
Loans to large companies	200	1	200
Loans to small companies	150	2.00	300
Total	500		550

The Bank's and *a fortiori* the EC's method of measuring the riskiness of assets seems unexceptionable. For example, for quoted securities, it bases the risk partly on the volatility of the price of this type of security, and partly on the 'thickness' of the market (if the Ruritanian stock exchange is a 'thin' one, then there may be problems in disposing of large holdings of Ruritanian Steel Shares, even if past quoted prices show little variation). Methods of measuring the risk of unquoted assets (that is loans) are equally pragmatic, but equally reasonable.

Where the Bank's method is controversial is in the assumption that the overall riskiness of a portfolio of assets can be measured in this way. For the statistician, the critique is simple: the Bank has committed the classic howler of assuming that the variance of the sum is equal to the sum of the variances (that is, it has ignored covariance). No one, of course, suggests that the Bank's experts are ignorant of elementary statistics – but they have chosen to behave as if they are.

For non-statisticians, the critique can best be understood using an example drawn from that riskiest of all activities, roulette. A European roulette wheel has 37 slots (1–36, plus zero), and when spun, a ball drops into one of the slots, the payouts to the gamblers being determined by which slot (number) this is: this example considers three bets:

54

A: 36,000 lire on high (19–35)
B: 36,000 lire on low (1–18)
C: 2,000 lire on zero

The first bet will be lost if either zero or any number between 1 and 18 appears. However, if any number between 19 and 36 appears, the gambler will receive his stake of 36,000 lire, plus winnings of 36,000 lire (that is 72,000 lire). The second bet will produce similar results, with a return of 72,000 lire if a number between 1 and 18 appears, but it will lose if either zero or 19–36 turns up. Finally, the 2,000 lire bet on zero will be lost, unless zero turns up; however, if zero does turn up, the gambler receives the stake (2,000 lire), plus winnings of 70,000 lire (35–1 is paid on a bet on a single number).

Each of the above three bets is highly risky, the third exceptionally so. However, the combination is riskless! Whichever number turns up, the gambler will receive 72,000 (from B if 1–18 turns up, A if 19–36 appears and from C if zero occurs).

Of course, the gambler has staked 74,000 lire to ensure a return of 72,000 whatever happens, so it is an unlikely combination; however, it is conceivable – for example if one were given complimentary chips and had to gamble them to convert them into cashable ones, or if gambling to impress others. More important, the example illustrates the two criticisms made of the Bank's methods:

1. The overall riskiness of a portfolio (in this case 3 bets) may be less than the riskiness of any component.
2. The addition of a very risky investment (the zero bet) may reduce the riskiness of the overall portfolio.

The counterpart argument in the real world often involves the use of forward dealing, futures, options, etc. as means of reducing overall risk (Gowland, 1990, pp. 65–7).

To summarize, *1992* involves a number of policy initiatives including the abolition of exchange control, the ERM of the EMS, country of origin regulation of financial markets and in consequence probably harmonized regulation. In the rest of this chapter I will explore the effects on two areas: demand management and the protection of depositors.

In this section I wish to explore how much freedom will be left to national governments after *1992* to choose the targets and instruments of macroeconomic policy. The most obvious constraints upon such choices stem from membership of the ERM of the EMS. A commitment to maintain an (adjustable) exchange rate parity *ipso facto* debars the discretionary use of the exchange rate as a tool of macroeconomic policy, for other purposes. Governments notably in the UK have frequently used the exchange rate to influence inflation and unemployment. A high exchange rate reduces inflation and a lower one reduces unemployment in the medium-term. Figure 3.1 illustrates the effect of a depreciation of the currency, in which the economy concerned is assumed to be a small one in the trade theory sense, that is unable to influence world prices. Hence all firms in the economy and by extension the economy itself are price takers at the world price experienced in terms of local currency. If the world price of a leet is $1 and the exchange rate $2 = £1 the UK price of a leet will be 50p. The UK producer will face a horizontal marginal revenue at this price so its optimal output will be q_1. If the exchange rate now falls to $1.50 = £1, the new world price of a leet will be 66p. Optimal output is now q_2, so the depreciation has increased UK output and so reduced unemployment. UK prices have, however, risen by 33 per cent. The price of inputs both imported and domestically produced will, however, rise *pari passu*. In addition real wages are lower and marginal value product higher so there must be a rise in wages. Both these effects will cause the marginal cost curve to shift upwards until it reaches MC_N and output returns to its original level. An appreciation of the exchange rate will reduce inflationary pressure at a cost in the short-term in terms of output.

One may argue the relevance of this model. Most producers are influenced by the price of imports – Fiat and BAe must consider the price of a BMW (and of each other) in fixing the price of a Lancia or a Rover but they scarcely face a horizontal marginal revenue curve. However, the mechanism has been incorporated into all modern macroeconomic models from international monetarism to the Scandinavian open economy Keynesian model. This reflects the fact that it captures an important feature of a modern medium-size currency like Germany, the UK or Italy without being the whole truth. The implications of this

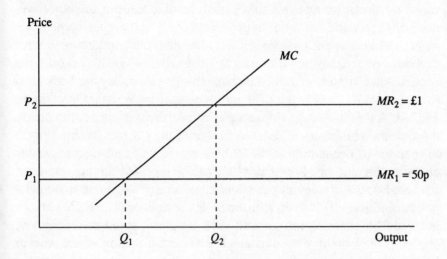

Figure 3.1
The effect of the exchange rate on the economy

a) Short term

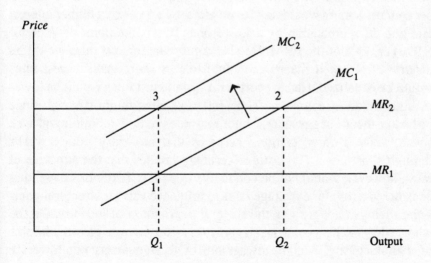

b) Long term

analysis go beyond the abandonment of a particular instrument of macroeconomic policy. *The model also implies that the price level will be determined only by the world price and the exchange rate.* If the ERM debars movement of the exchange rate then a country's price level will be determined by world prices, as in the gold standard.

In general, membership of the ERM rules out short-term discretionary use of the exchange rate as a policy instrument to achieve any objective, not just output and inflation. In practice, however, there are some other objectives that might be appropriate other than those intertwined with exchange rate management itself (considered below) such as short-term capital flows. In some circumstances exchange rate policy has been used to achieve other usually political ends – notably by Weimar Germany in 1922–3. A Reichsmark collapse was engineered, it is alleged, to create the appearance of chaos in order to pressurise the UK into forcing France to abandon its occupation of the Ruhr. Nevertheless such circumstances are both rare and, one hopes, not likely to be repeated. In the long-term the ERM does not rule out the selection of an exchange rate to achieve policy objectives. However, adjustment is constrained. The ERM parities can only be changed infrequently and by small amounts. Moreover, continual movement of the exchange rate in one direction would have to be offset by a higher or lower interest rate than the European average. Otherwise the currency would be too unattractive or too attractive to be held in equilibrium quantities – a regular downward movement of, say, 5 per cent per annum would have to be offset by a 5 per cent higher interest rate and an appreciation by a lower one. This is the point of Walters' (1990) critique of the ERM. He also argues that interest rates would be distorted from their macro economic role as *short-term* interest rates would be equalized. Hence short-term real interest rates would be lower in high inflation countries. Thus inflation rates might diverge since orthodox theory suggests that high real rates reduce inflation and *vice versa*. Thus *Walters' critique* assumes that monetary policy works through short-rates. The critique certainly implies that the structure of rates, however, would not be conducive to policy. Textbooks have long considered a role for exchange rates to influence various structural goals – the savings rate, growth, the sectoral distribution of industry. On the whole a low exchange rate *ceteris paribus* raises savings, growth, the size of manufacturing, and the ownership of foreign assets but lowers a country's standard of living. It is probably the case that such models have influenced planners in a number of European countries, especially France, but less clear that such analysis is still relevant even in the absence of the ERM. Indeed, I would argue that in practice such models were too abstract to ever have provided a useful guide to policy.

It is normal to state the above propositions about the relationship between the exchange rate and the price level in a more positive form – the ERM replaces internal discipline (such as that imposed by a money supply target) with a more effective external discipline. External discipline in theory constrains a country's inflation rate to the world rate – in practice in the ERM the German rate. Given that the model above is an over simplification, however, it seems more appropriate to analyse the precise nature of the discipline in reality, that is the constraints placed upon macroeconomic management. They can, for example, be seen in French policy in the 1980s notably in the abandonment of Mitterand's reflationary experiment in 1983. Such constraints of course may be regarded as good or bad. Mrs Thatcher argues that they interfere with national sovereignty and democracy – ironically a traditional left-wing line. Many in the British financial community welcome them: German central bankers have a better record than British politicians. Whether they are regarded as good or bad it is nevertheless important to examine their nature. After all the ERM exists and even at a normative level the nature of a constraint may influence its desirability.

The actual constraint placed upon a country is that it must be willing to exchange its currency for that of other members at an agreed level – the lower end of the prescribed range. It is one of the features of the ERM that the onus of adjustment is put squarely on the country whose currency is moving towards the lower point of its prescribed range, not upon one which is appreciating.

This constraint bites whenever there is a crisis of confidence in a currency, in other words when speculators feel that it is likely to fall in value. In these circumstances a central bank is likely to be forced to buy its currency in very large quantities. These are likely to exceed its own resources of foreign currency as well as what it can obtain via the ECF and the BIS. This possibility is reinforced by the fact that the ERM provides a one-way option because it is usually clear that a currency can only move in one direction if its parity is adjusted. Hence speculators selling a currency short face only small certain costs: they do not have to allow for the risk of a sharp upward movement. Contrawise with a floating system the authorities can let the rate move downwards to the point where this risk is recreated and so choke-off speculation. Moreover such a downward move is likely to make the currency seem attractive to someone. Hence protection of a suspect currency is much simpler and requires less reserves with a floating system than with one of adjustable parities. This is especially so with the ERM as political constraints mean that the process of adjusting parities usually takes several weeks and is often signalled by, for example, a meeting of EC finance ministers. In short exchange rate management would be extremely difficult under the ERM. It is therefore clear that membership of the ERM would periodically pose insuperable problems to members unless reinforced by other instruments. In principle a country faced with a crisis of confidence can do any of three things:

(a) *leave the ERM*

This seems a futile and self-defeating policy. One assumes that the EC's future health depends upon members not popping in and out of the ERM every few months. Presumably the ERM could not survive long in such circumstances. In fact the UK did join and leave the previous incarnation of the ERM (the EMU – European Monetary Union) in 1972. The resulting fiasco was not only humiliating and expensive for the UK but set European integration back for several years. Other countries were forced to follow the UK's example and the whole idea of economic and monetary unity lay dormant until revised by Jenkins (as Commission President), Schmidt and D'Estaing in 1977–8.

(b) *use direct controls to control speculation*

To a considerable but unquantifiable extent, France and Italy were able to remain members of ERM from 1979–89 only because they were able to use exchange control to support ERM membership. Belgium used the similar device of a two-tier exchange rate, one for speculative and one for trade purposes. Now these are no longer possible.

(c) *adjust macroeconomic policy so as to convince wealth holders that the currency is worth holding*

Such a policy adjustment might be merely a hike in interest rates. At least on some occasions, however, a more significant readjustment will be necessary. France had to abandon the reflation experiment that followed

60

President Mitterand's election in 1981 for exactly this reason. Such adjustments were common under Bretton Woods – the UK 1964–70 being a classic example (Beckerman, 1972). Exchange rate pressures may cause policy adjustments under a floating rate (Herriot in France, 1924 and Blum-Daladier (Popular Front) in 1936–8 being well-documented examples although the UK 1974–9 seems a more modern example). Nevertheless, such adjustment would be more common and more violent under the ERM because capital flows are so much larger thanks to the Eurocurrency market and other manifestations of financial innovation.

The usual answer to this problem is that macroeconomic coordination would be necessary. In other words, that macroeconomic policy would be such that crises of confidence would not arise. This is sometimes stated – for example by Mrs Thatcher – in terms of similar inflation rates. In point of fact this is neither sufficient nor necessary but mistakes a symptom for a cause. The requirement is that domestic credit expansion (DCE) growth in each country is at a level determined by the size of the economy and various structural parameters – see McKinnon (1979) Dornbusch (1980) or Williamson (1983). In an open economy the growth of the money supply is equal to DCE plus an overseas effect which is approximately equal to the balance of payments surplus – see for example Gowland (1991). Thus if a country has a balance of payments surplus its money supply grows faster than DCE whereas a deficit reduces monetary growth below DCE. This ensures stability since the expansion by surplus countries generates both a higher income and inflation both of which erode surpluses and *vice versa* for a deficit. Indeed a DCE target is usually thought to be the next logical stage of economic and monetary union.

Having examined the constraint it is necessary to look at the objectives that remain to macroeconomic policy under the ERM. The most important would be output and employment. Membership of the ERM does not guarantee full employment, indeed the reverse. The deflation imposed as necessary to eliminate a balance of payments deficit (by the DCE target) might well cause unemployment. The optimum currency area literature pioneered by McKinnon (1963) demonstrated that fixing the exchange rate between two economies will increase average unemployment in at least one of them. Indeed unemployment arises in the same way and for the same reason as in a region of a single economy. Hence the stress on regional policy within the EC, see chapter 7.

To summarize the argument, a member of the ERM would have to rely on external discipline to control inflation. DCE growth would be constrained to the level necessary to maintain the exchange rate parity. DCE is basically equal to

the PSBR (Public Sector Borrowing Requirement)
+ Bank Loans to the Non-bank Private Sector (private credit)
− Non-bank Private Sector Loans to the Public Sector.

The PSBR is a definition of the budget deficit being equal to

Government Spending
− Taxation
− Asset Sales
+ Government Loans to Other Sectors (these include nationalised industry losses).

Given the constraint on the size of DCE, any objectives of macroeconomic policy such as unemployment would have to be met by adjusting the components of DCE or the PSBR. For example, government spending could be increased but only if credit were reduced or assets sold, taxes raised or some other adjustment made to ensure that not only would the government expenditure be financed but the DCE target met. The difference is that a budget deficit can be financed by borrowing from the domestic (non-bank) sector, from domestic banks or from overseas. The latter two would not reduce DCE. Only expenditure financed by borrowing from the non-bank private sector satisfies both the DCE and government finance constraints. Hence deficits financed by borrowing from other sources have to be accompanied by reductions in private credit. A government that wished to increase its expenditure (or reduce taxation) to reduce unemployment would therefore face much greater constraints than at present. A fall in output would be expected to raise nationalised industry losses, raise the cost of unemployment pay and reduce taxation. All would raise DCE. Hence faced with rising unemployment, the DCE constraint might imply deflation while Keynesian remedies suggested reflation.

To compound the problem of discretionary changes, when DCE targets are introduced in the mid-1990s it will be against a background of widely divergent structural budget deficits. Belgium and Italy both have a PSBR of between 15 and 20 per cent of GDP. Germany has one of 4 per cent and the UK a surplus of 1–2 per cent. In the UK's case this is accompanied by massive credit-growth which results in a very high DCE. At the least such aberrant patterns would impose much greater costs on the countries concerned than hitherto. However, it is necessary to see if they are even feasible.

To state the problem, an above EC-average budget deficit, either structural or discretionary, has to be matched by one of

(a) above-average asset sales
(b) above-average sales of public sector debt to the domestic non-bank sector
(c) below-average growth of private sector credit.

Contrawise above-average growth of credit requires either (a) or (b) the budget deficit to be below average. Hence a repeat of the Barber boom (1971–3) or Lawson boom (1985–8) in the UK would also run into a DCE constraint. Even the normal rate of growth of credit in the UK poses problems. Given the relative size of the magnitudes in the UK one of (a) or (b) above would be necessary. In 1988, for example, credit grew by £70 billion, the budget surplus was £12 billion. To meet the probable level of an ERM DCE target a £35 billion adjustment would have been necessary.

All of (a), (b) and (c) above face problems. Asset sales would cause ideological problems for many governments who believe that certain industries and functions belong in the public sector. Moreover, even if the stock of public sector assets is sufficiently large, asset sales on the scale necessary would probably not be feasible for reasons of capital market indigestion. Even if they were the sale of, say, IRI[4] remove a further policy instrument in Italy where public sector investment has long been an instrument of macroeconomic and regional policy.

Debt sales to the domestic non-bank private sector are also restricted in size, especially in the absence of exchange control. Savers and institutions are likely to wish to hold a substantial and growing part of their assets abroad. Hence their appetite for domestic money-denominated securities will be limited and the public sector will not have a monopoly of such securities. Sales of index-linked and foreign currency securities will increase the maximum attainable level of debt sales to the non-bank domestic private sector. It is impossible to quantify the maxima for debt sales but one will exist so there will be a constraint on macroeconomic policy.

In principle, credit can be restrained by any of

(a) direct controls, rationing in some form such as ceilings
(b) higher interest rates
(c) reserve ratios.

All have problems. The problem of direct controls is evasion, that the ceiling creates an incentive to evade it profitably. Both off-balance sheet and offshore lending could be used given the absence of exchange control.

Many institutions grew up in London in the 1960s to evade ceilings on bank lending – secondary banks for example. They aimed to perform banking business in practice but in a legal form chosen so as not to be subject to the ceiling rather as clubs often fulfil the functions of pubs while evading the restrictions on them. Evasion of the UK ceilings on bank deposits in the 1970s also occurred but mainly in two other ways. One was *offshore banking,* as with the Eurocurrency market; the deposit was 'booked' to a foreign banking centre and any loan made from this branch (I can deposit money in a York bank and the amount be credited to an account with a branch in London or Paris. It is then said to be 'booked' to London or Paris). This was especially prevalent in the last few months of the ceiling, after the abolition of exchange control in November 1979. More generally, offshore banking can be used to evade a wide variety of controls on banks – reserve requirements, capital adequacy requirements, constraints on the quantity or type of lending. The implications of this for *EC-wide* regulation are fundamental but well outside the scope of this chapter.

Earlier in the 1970s, evasion of the 'corset' occurred via the 'bill leak' or letter of acceptance leak (named after a particular form of bill). Normally, without any controls, A deposits money with a bank and receives a security (a bank deposit in exchange). This is matched on the bank's balance sheet by a loan to B, who thereby obtains funds. Instead A may go into a bank and receive in exchange for his deposit not a claim on the bank but a bank-guaranteed claim on B (that is a bill of exchange). In reality all is the same; A has a security, B has his loan, the transaction has occurred because A trusts the bank, etc. However, legally A no longer has a deposit so the control has been evaded. This was often called disintermediation in the UK but is now usually termed *off-balance-sheet lending*. More generally, disintermediation and offshore banking can be used to evade a wide range of controls on banks – reserve requirements, constraints on the quantity or type of lending, and of current significance, capital adequacy ratios.

No doubt such problems are greater in the UK than they would be in France or Italy, with simpler institutional and more cohesive power structures. Nevertheless it would be rash to rely upon direct controls. Interest rate changes are slow-acting and would be constrained by their effect on exchange rates. Reserve ratios combine elements of both interest rates and direct controls (Gowland, 1991). Critically they can be evaded by both off-balance sheet lending and offshore lending, as argued above. For the reasons Pöhl of the Bundesbank has cast doubt upon whether they will be viable in the EC in future, 19 May 1990.

A textbook lists a large number of instruments of demand management – budgetary policy, exchange rate policy, a plethora of instruments of financial policy and direct controls, rationing etc. While only the latter is explicitly restricted by *1992* the above analysis suggests that all will be affected.

In a sentence *1992* reduces both the scope of and instruments available to macroeconomic policy. The implications are less clear – should the EC having swallowed the camel of *1992* go straight to the gnat of political union since little effective sovereignty remains to member states after *1992*? Is political union or even the Delors scheme for monetary union unnecessary? Should elements of *1992* be reconsidered?

3.3 DEPOSITOR PROTECTION AND BANK SAFETY AFTER *1992*

Almost from their emergence central banks have sought both to reduce the risk of bank failure and to ameliorate the consequences of any failures that do occur. Bank failure is likely to reduce overall confidence in the banking system and indeed in the financial system. It may threaten the solvency of other banks, directly or though a contingency plan induced by fear that other banks may fail. The bank's customers may suffer either if loans and investments are liquidated or called in or if depositors lose part of the value of their deposit. In modern textbooks and legislation the interests of the latter are often listed as a separate objective: *depositor protection.* Central banks take different approaches to the problem. The Banca d'Italia relies on the Banking Act 1936 which virtually precludes bank failure – none has failed since – reinforced by voluntary deposit insurance, which seems somewhat superfluous. The 1936 Act effectively combines restrictions on bank activity, to reduce risk, with a guarantee of central bank assistance if a bank gets into trouble. However, such an approach greatly restricts competition so other central banks select different positions on the competition/risk of insolvency trade-off. The US authorities have since 1933 relied on a continuation of compulsory deposit insurance to protect depositors (up to $100,000) with a liberal approach to competition. Deposit insurance guarantees repayment of deposits by the insurer in the event of default.

Bank failures have been fairly frequent in the USA – about 10–20 per annum in most of the last 50 years although there have been 200–300 per annum in recent years. In many cases, the Federal Deposit Insurance Corporation (FDIC) assumes responsibility for all the liabilities of a bank ('purchase and assumption') so all the depositors are repaid, not just small ones. In practice this is often cheaper than liquidation but intensifies the problem of moral hazard, below. Most European central banks select some intermediate position which involves some risk, some guarantee fund or deposit insurance to protect small depositors and a significant but not unrestricted amount of competition.

1992 involves a significant amount of liberalisation of banking. This is both a direct objective of the Community and an indirect consequence of the competition in laxity and abolition of exchange control discussed above. Regulations would both be more liberal and easier to evade. Since the analysis in section 2 is as relevant to micro economic as macro economic issues. The potential dangers of such deregulation are well-illustrated by the Savings and Loans (S and Ls) Association Fiasco in the USA; S and Ls or thrifts are the US equivalent of UK building societies and similar to Cassa di Risparmio in the USA (except that their principal investment is personal sector mortgages). In 1979–82 they were

66

deregulated; the authorities relied on deposit insurance to protect investors. By the beginning of 1990 the Federal authorities had paid out $40 billion to depositors of failed thrifts. More seriously the Federal authorities had had to take over half (500) of the remaining thrifts because they were insolvent, in half these cases because of criminal fraud, in half because of incompetence or imprudence. The cost of meeting the deficiency was estimated by the General Accounting Office at $500 billion. Given that most of the EC uses deposit insurance in some form or other it is important to examine the causes of the disaster.

The main problem with any form of insurance is moral hazard – those insured change their behaviour in a counter-productive manner. For example, in the case of fire insurance those insured may become more careless when smoking or less likely to check that televisions have been unplugged like most common cause of fires. In the case of depositors, insurance means that they place funds heedlessly without considering the riskiness of the institution – why should they? In consequence institutions obtain funds without paying the market price of the risk they assume. Moreover in any case there is an asymmetry of reward. If an S and L invests in a risky asset and the gamble pays off, all the return accrues to the owners (the depositor receives only a fixed return). If it does not come off then the consequence is bankruptcy and some of the costs are borne by the insurers. Once losses have been made the incentive is to take risks which if they come off save the institution. If they do there is no private cost to the owner in a bigger deficiency nor a cost to depositors only to the insurers. These considerations were reinforced by the opportunity to the criminal to obtain deposits and steal them directly or indirectly, by loans to companies they owned.

What lessons does this have for the European Community? The first is that it is now impossible to restrict the maximum size of the deposit insured. Depositors can split a large deposit up into a number of small ones, all below the insurance limit. Alternatively they can use brokered deposits, that is pay a broker to break up the large deposit for them. The second lesson is confirmation of a traditional proposition, that deposit insurance does not remove the need for regulation. Instead it reinforces it because deposit insurance encourages reckless behaviour. Recklessness needs to be constrained – hence the need for regulation. However, such regulation is probably no longer enforceable, for the reasons discussed above. Certainly any EC decision to use deposit insurance requires the most careful consideration. Risks will remain even if an improved version is adopted with risk-related premia and a significant co-insurance element (only a proportion of deposits are insured). At a national level the risks are still greater. One solution is the UK one – put a maximum on the amount paid out each year and scale-down all claims if they exceed this amount. However, political pressure may make it hard to stand by the limit and, in any case, it destroys much of the purpose of insurance.

Although the systems of regulating financial markets which evolved over time in the member states of the EC differed significantly from country to country, the systems were always based on three common assumptions:

1. A closed market, that is a market in which the number and operations of the agents offering financial services was relatively constant – that is there was relatively little entry or exit. In many ways, this is similar to Baumol's concept of an (almost) perfectly uncontestable market (see above). In part this was achieved by regulation but banking was much less contestable in the 1950s than in the 1980s because of the role of branch networks and the nature of the credit market. The effect of this was that the central bank or other regulatory agency knew a great deal about the agents operating in the markets and could develop a system to deal with a known quantity.
2. Each agent pursued a limited and constant range of activities.
3. Each agent operated predominantly in one country.

The combination of the first and second assumption was that it was then possible to distinguish sharply banking from other activities. The authorities could then impose a 'ring fence' around banking and carefully segregate it from other activities. The authorities regulated banking much more carefully and supervised it more closely than other activities. Banks were not only 'special' in the eyes of the economist, but had a special regulatory system developed by the central bank. Moreover, the traditional theory of the regulation and supervision of banking laid special emphasis on the function of 'lender-of-last-resort'. The lender-of-last-resort was largely intended to cope with a specific problem (in addition to its role in the operation of macro-monetary policy); this was to sustain a financial institution which was basically solvent but facing temporary liquidity problems. A bank may fail for two reasons: insolvency and illiquidity. A bank is insolvent if the value of its assets is less than the value of its liabilities. A bank fails through liquidity problems if it cannot repay a depositor on demand. A bank that is solvent may be illiquid if some or all of its assets cannot be sold. The classic 'run on the bank' arises from a liquidity crisis.

Classic central banking was supposed to deal only with a liquidity crisis. In practice, liquidity and solvency may be interdependent; it may be that a bank would be solvent if given sufficient time to realize its assets, but that the short-term value of its assets causes a solvency as well as liquidity problem. Bagehot (1965), Hawtry (1932), Sayers (1957 edn) and other central banking theorists have argued that this was also a reason for central bank intervention.[5] The central bank would be prepared to purchase assets from this bank, or otherwise provide liquidity to enable the institution to remain in existence. In practice, of course, this orthodox view was not always applied and, in any case, liquidity and solvency problems were often interrelated. From Bagehot onwards, theorists of central banking wrestled with this problem. Bagehot (1965) suggested that the test should be whether a bank was solvent if its assets were valued at normal prices, that is not at the temporarily depressed levels which prevailed in a 'panic'. If it passed the test, the central bank should act as lender-of-last-resort. This test is entirely subjective (what is 'normal'?) and, in practice, central bankers have to act quickly, so it is difficult to appraise a bank's solvency in the time available; and, *mutatis mutandis,* it is even harder for other financial institutions. Hence the 'lender-of-last-resort' role may not have been as clear, in practice, as either the pronouncements of central bankers or the classic textbooks (Sayers, 1957; Hawtrey, 1932; etc.) suggested.

The third assumption led to the development of the 'native principle', whereby each central bank was supposed to assume responsibility for the activities of its own banks, whether at home or abroad. Thus, for example, if a British bank established a branch in Italy, it would still be the responsibility of the Bank of England. Of course, the British bank has to observe Italian regulations on its Italian business. However, prudential responsibility was shared by the Banca d'Italia and the Bank of England; and in the event of default by this bank, the Bank of England would have been left to pick up the bill.

The logic underlying the native principle was that despite its international operations, the great bulk of both the assets and liabilities of the British bank would still be British ones; moreover, if it were to go bankrupt, nearly all the other consequences would be felt within the UK. Hence it was therefore quite reasonable for the Bank of England to assume this responsibility. It is fair to say that the 'native principle' was never fully accepted by all central banks and, to some extent, evolved and emerged during the 1960s; nevertheless, the native principle was regarded in the early 1970s as the cornerstone whereby the traditional system could accommodate international banking. Country of origin shares many features in common with the nature principle. A British bank operating in Italy is the responsibility of the Bank of England not the *Banca d'Italia* in both cases.

It may be a cliché to say that the financial system has been changing rapidly in recent years and has now become a truly global market-place. Nevertheless, however often these and similar phrases are repeated, it is still true that innovation and internationalization have wrecked the assumptions upon which the traditional system of regulation was based. Internationalization has meant that the native principle is no longer operable. The defects of this principle were first exposed by the collapse of Banco Ambrosiano in 1982. An attempt was made to revive the 'native principle' in 1982; see the discussion of the Concordat which embodied the native principle in the *Bank of England Quarterly Bulletin*, vol. 23, no. 1, March 1983, 1–5 (speech by W.P. Cooke). In particular, it is no longer the case that the bulk of any large bank's business is done with residents of a particular country. More generally, regulators have to face up to the problems caused by innovation and internationalization for country of origin regulation. It seems unlikely that tax payers funds can be used to bail-out banks if a substantial fraction of the depositors are citizens of other countries.

Hence, there seem to be problems in reliance on any of the traditional methods of depositor protection – deposit insurance, tight regulation or bail-outs. Community-wide solutions (or wider international cooperation) are attractive as with capital adequacy ratios but many of the problems above still arise – for example offshore banking can be used to evade Community regulations in the absence of exchange control.

NOTES

1. See Hitiris' chapter (nine) in Gowland 1990a. The bands may be ±2¼ percent or ±6 percent. Parity adjustment is now less frequent than in the early years of the ERM, established in January 1979.
2. The ECU is a basket of currencies, that if its value is equal to the sum of x French francs, if pence sterling etc. See the discussion in Hitiris, cited in note 1.
3. IRI – a state-holding company founded by Mussolini whose acronym translates roughly as Industrial Reconstruction Institute; see Holland (1972). Italy is discussed at length in chapter 7 of this book.
4. See Gowland (1991 and references therein, especially Bordo (1990).

REFERENCES

Bagehot (1965) "Lombard Street", reprinted in *Collected Works, The Economist.*

Barrow, R.J. *et al* (1988), *Black Monday and the Future of Financial Markets*, Dow Jones – Irwin, New York.

Baumol, W.J. *et al* (1982) *Contestable Markets and the Theory of Industrial Structure*, Harcourt, Brace Jovanovich, New York.

Beckerman, W. (ed.) (1972) *The Labour Government's Economic Record 1964–70*, Duckworth.

Bordo, M. (1990) "The Leaders of Last Resort: Alternative Views and Historical Experience", *Economic Review,* Federal Reserve Bank of Richmond, Vol.71/1 (Jan/Feb) pp.18–29.

Cosci, S. (1991) *Credit Rationing*, Dartmouth, Aldershot.

Davies, G. and Davies J. (1984) "The Revolution in Monopoly Theory", *Lloyds Bank Review,* No.153 (July) pp.38–52.

Di Cagno, D. (1990) *The Regulation of Banks,* Avebury, Aldershot, Hants.

Dornbusch, R. (1980) *Open Economy Macroeconomics,* Basic Books, New York.

Gowland, D.H. (1990) *The Regulation of Financial Markets in the 1990s,* Edward Elgar, Aldershot.

Gowland, D.H. (1991) *Monetary Control in Theory and Practice,* Routledge, London.

Gowland, D.H. (1979) *Modern Economic Analysis,* Butterworths, Sevenoaks.

Gowland, D.H. (1990a) *Understanding Macroeconomics,* Edward Elgar, Aldershot.

Gowland, D.H. (1988) "Il Processo di deregolamentazione finanziaria alla luce jella recente crise dei mercati borststici mondiali", *Economia Italiana,* Banco D'Roma, No.3, pp.389–410.

Hawtrey, R.G. (1932) *The Art of Central Banking,* Oxford University Press, Oxford.

Holland, S. (1972) (ed) *The State as Entrepreneur,* Weidenfeld, Nicholson.

King, M. (1989) *International Harmonization of the Regulation of Financial Markets,* LSE Financial Markets Group (Special Paper No.19), London.

Llewellyn D. (1988b) "Integration of European Financial Markets" in *Economia Italiana,* Banco Di Roma, No.3.

Llewellyn, D.T. (1990) "Structural Change in the British Financial System" in Kaufman, G. (ed.) *The Banking Structure in Major Countries,* Federal Reserve Bank of Chicago, Chicago.

McKinnon, R.I. (1963) "Optimum Currency Areas", *American Economic Review,* Vol.53, pp.717–25.

McKinnon, R.I. (1979) *Money in International Exchange,* Oxford University Press, Oxford.

Sayers, R.S. (1957) *Central Banking After Bagehot,* Oxford University Press, Oxford.

Shoup, C.S. (ed) (1967) *Fiscal Harmonization in Common Markets* (2 vols), Columba University Press, New York.

Walters, A.A. (1990) *Sterling in Danger,* Fontana/Collins, London.

Welsh, J. (1981) *The Regulation of Banks in the Member States of the EEC,* Graham and Trotman, London.

Welsh, J. (1981) *The Regulation of Banks in the Member States of the EEC,* Graham and Trotman, London.

Williamson, J. (1983) *The Open Economy and the World Economy,* Basic Books, New York.

4 Tax harmonisation in the European Community[1]

Andrew M. Jones

4.1 INTRODUCTION

Harmonisation of indirect taxes plays a central role in the European Community's plans for 1992, and the Commission's proposals are often presented as a precondition for completion of the internal market. Nevertheless the actual progress towards these objectives has been fraught with political obstacles; some proposals have stagnated or disappeared from the agenda, while others have evolved according to political expediency. Any attempt to provide an up to date survey of the proposals, and the debate they have stimulated, is therefore a precarious undertaking (section 2 gives a brief outline of the current position). However, one certainty is that the issue has attracted considerable attention from economists.

The purpose of this chapter is to show how economic concepts and results have been applied to the issue of tax harmonisation and, in certain cases, how the issue has stimulated new developments in the economic analysis of taxation. The starting point is to ask whether Community intervention in Members States' tax policies is appropriate and, if so, how should it be evaluated? These broad issues are discussed in section 3 which outlines the normative criteria for assessing European tax policy.

The main focus of the chapter is on indirect taxation. This is the area where EC policy has had most impact on Member States and which has stimulated most debate in the economic literature. This debate is divided into two broad issues: reform of the tax structure and approximation of tax rates. With the former, attention has focussed on the principles of international taxation; in particular whether the EC should shift from the destination to the origin principle (or its variants, the restricted origin principle and the common market/tax union principle (CMP/TUP)). The debate over tax rates can be summarised as uniformity versus diversity; this raises questions ranging from the abstract concerns of optimal tax theory to practical problems of tax administration. International tax principles are discussed in section 4, while section 5 looks at the role of economic analysis in the uniformity/diversity debate.

The debates over tax principles and uniformity of tax rates come together in the central question of whether harmonisation is a necessary condition for completion of the internal market. The belief that it is a precondition has informed official EC thinking on the issue (see, for example, Guieu and Bonnet, 1987), but has been challenged by a number of commentators (see, for example, Cnossen, 1989; Smith, 1990), and by some Member States (see, for example, Brooke, 1989) for the view of the UK Government). Section 6 looks at the arguments for and against recent EC proposals and at the counter-proposals put forward by their critics.

It is clear from recent contributions to the literature, that the focus of the policy debate is swinging towards direct taxation (see, for example, Gammie and Robinson, 1989), and in particular to corporate taxation. A full discussion of direct taxation is beyond the scope of the current chapter.[2] The central issue raised by taxation of income from financial or industrial capital is the choice between the *source principle* (where production takes place or profits originate) and the *residence principle* (according to the legal residence of the parent company or shareholder). A move to the source principle could lead to a flight of financial capital, which is a highly mobile tax base particularly after exchange controls have been removed, in response to differential tax rates. As a result high tax countries could experience a loss in their tax base; this danger has clear parallels with the possible *competition in laxity* in financial markets associated with the move from *host country* to *country of origin* regulation, as described by David Gowland in chapter 3 of this volume. Direct taxation of income from capital raises other problems; the definition of profits, and hence the tax base, is less straightforward than

74

indirect taxes, and with the anticipated growth of pan-European enterprises this is complicated by the problems of allocating their profits among the different countries of operation.

In general, direct taxation of labour and property income has received very little attention in the harmonisation debate. This fits in with the view that the urgency for progress on harmonisation is a positive function of the mobility of the tax base. For instance, Sorenson (1990) describes a spectrum running from financial capital, where he argues harmonisation is urgent, through industrial capital, goods, labour, and land or property. The rest of this chapter concentrates primarily on goods and assesses the economic arguments surrounding indirect tax harmonisation.

4.2 A BRIEF REVIEW OF PROGRESS TOWARDS HARMONISATION

Key events in the historical development of the EC's tax policy are summarised in the appendix, which makes it clear that there has often been a gulf between the plans made by the Commission and the practical response of Member States. A sign of the controversy caused by the issue is the so-called *Luxembourg compromise,* which means that taxation is one of the few areas of European policy that still requires unanimity in the Council of Ministers (see Jenkins, 1989). This section gives a brief outline of the current set of proposals for approximation of tax rates within the Community.

4.2.1 Value-Added Tax

Prior to 1967 most of the Member States had turnover taxes based on the *cascade* system, where a full ad valorem tax is paid on each transaction during the production process. The main distortion caused by this tax mechanism is to encourage vertical integration among firms simply to minimise their tax burden. Under VAT, tax is only paid on value-added and is therefore "neutral with regard to the structure of economic activity" (Harrop, 1989). The cascade system was also accused of providing a hidden subsidy to exporters. When making border adjustments it was often difficult to account for the value of the goods at each previous

75

transaction. The VAT system reduces the possibility for this kind of evasion. So, while it is easy to be cynical about European achievement in harmonising tax rates, the achievement of a common system of VAT and the substantial agreement on a common basis (despite wrangles over zero-rating) should not be under-estimated.

As regards rates of VAT, the current position of the Commission is that there should be a reduced rate of 4–9%, along with a minimum level for the standard rate (see, for example, Gammie and Robinson, 1989, p.4; Curwen, 1990, p.125; Bull.EC, 5–89, p.8), it is likely that what this minimum will be 15%; this would allow for the high standard rate of 22% in Denmark. The move towards tax minima, as opposed to target rates, is in line with arguments put forward by many critics of the need for harmonisation of Community rates (see section 6 below). The proposals also allow Member States to retain some zero-rated goods that are eligible under the common basis although this would not include children's clothing; a contentious issue in the UK. The Cockfield plan for a computerised clearing house to reallocate tax revenue between Member States has been modified in response to a hostile political reception. The current proposal is to use aggregate overseas trade statistics to calculate the necessary compensating transfers of revenue between national tax authorities.

When reviewing the progress on harmonisation of rates it is tempting to conclude that it is the Commissions proposals that have evolved towards the actual rates, rather than vice versa. This view is illustrated by Figure 4.1.

Similar signs of resistance to change have surfaced in disagreements between the Commission and the Council (Economic and Financial Affairs) on the move to the origin principle for VAT collection. At the meeting of 13 November 1989 the Council took the position that while a move to a uniform system of taxation based on the origin principle remains the "medium term" objective, for a "limited period" member states should maintain a destination based system "under the conditions obtaining in that country" (Bull.EC 11–89). In response the Commission has expressed reservations about progress on tax policy and scepticism about the "transitional nature" of the Council's plan, arguing that the Council "has for its part not yet shown the political will necessary for tax frontiers to be abolished by January 1 1993" (Bull.EC 11–89). The overall picture is of a continuation of the destination principle into the

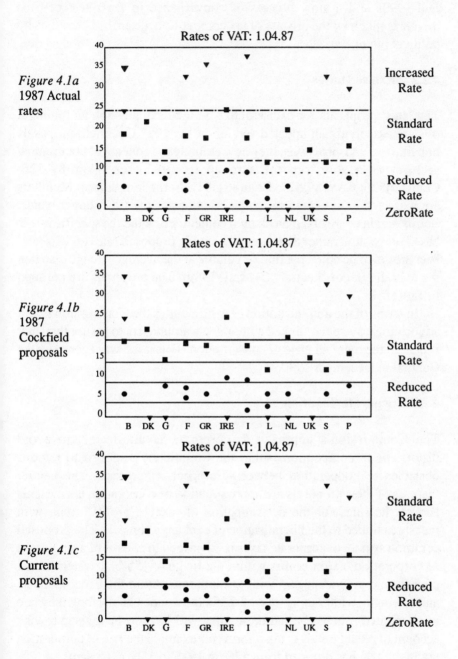

Figure 4.1a
1987 Actual rates

Rates of VAT: 1.04.87

Increased Rate

Standard Rate

Reduced Rate
ZeroRate

Figure 4.1b
1987 Cockfield proposals

Rates of VAT: 1.04.87

Standard Rate

Reduced Rate

Figure 4.1c
Current proposals

Rates of VAT: 1.04.87

Standard Rate

Reduced Rate
ZeroRate

Source: Powell (1988), Curwen (1990)

mid-1990s and a slow process of convergence in tax rates, perhaps driven as much by the process of tax competition, described below, as by political intent.

4.2.2 Excise Duties

The latest proposals for excise duties on tobacco, alcohol, and mineral oils are essentially an updated version of the 1987 Cockfield proposals but, like the VAT proposals, they now embody the concept of tax minima, at least as a short-run measure up to 1992 (see, Com(89)525; Com(89)526; Com(89)527; Com(89)551). In the longer term Members are expected to converge on target rates or narrow (2%) target bands. Spirits and beer are taxed on alcohol content. For wine the specific rate is based on volume rather than strength, but the proposed rates on wine and beer are set to be equal per litre of volume at the average strength "so that the overall effect is neutral" (Powell, 1989). The proposals are outlined in Table 4.1.

In terms of the administration of excise duties the Commission is still advocating a system of linked authorised warehousers to ensure that duty is paid in the member state of consumption. This issue was agreed by the Council in December 1990.

4.2.3 Corporate Taxation

The Commission's approach to corporate taxation aims to avoid distortions to competition within the Community and also to remove obstacles to cooperation between European enterprises. The central features of their proposals are approximation of corporation tax systems and of the rules for the determination of taxable profits, along with measures linked to the liberalisation of exchange controls. The proposed common system of corporate taxes is envisaged to consist of a single rate of corporation tax on profits within the range 45–55%, a system of tax credits on dividends, again with a single rate within the band 45–55%, and a single withholding tax of 25% on dividends. Before they are implemented it is likely that these rates will have to be revised to take account of recent trends in tax reform (for example the rate of corporation tax in the UK has dropped from 52% in 1975 to 35% at present).

Table 4.1

Proposals for Excise Duty

Cigarettes:	VAT + ad valorem excise	Minimum	45
	(as % of retail price)	Target	54
	Specific (ECU/1000)	Minimum	15
		Target	21.5
Cigars and Cigarillos:	Tax as % of retail price	Minimum	25
		Target	34-36
Smoking Tobacco:		Minimum	50
		Target	54-56
Snuff and Chewing Tobacco:		Minimum	37
		Target	41-43

Pure Spirits:	Minimum	1118 ECU per hectolitre of pure alcohol
	Target	Approx. 1400
Beer:	Minimum	0.748 ECU per hectolitre per degree plato, for average strength of 12.5 gives 9.35 ECU
	Target	Approx 18 ECU, for average strength
Still Wine:	Minimum 9.35 ECU per hectolitre of wine	
	Target	Approx. 18

Leaded Petrol:	ECU per 1000Lt	Minimum	337
Unleaded petrol:		Minimum	287

Source: Com(89) 525, 526, 527, 551

4.3 NORMATIVE CRITERIA FOR EUROPEAN TAX POLICY

4.3.1 Is EC Intervention Appropriate?

In the debate over tax harmonisation it is common to take the rationale for EC intervention for granted, and to concentrate on the desirability of particular proposals for tax structures and rates. However, Smith (1990) raises the more fundamental question of what is the appropriate division of responsibility for tax policy between the Community and the individual Member States. He argues that, in terms of economic efficiency, there should be a general presumption in favour of decentralisation of political decision-making. The reasoning is that localised decisions are more likely to reflect local or individual preferences, and that a special case must be made for centralisation. This suggests that there may be an optimal assignment of functions between local, national, and Community tiers of government (see, for example, Helm and Smith, 1989)).

A related perspective on this issue is described by Cnossen (1989). He looks at tax coordination in terms of *public choice theory* and argues that harmonisation may be compared to cartelisation. Member States may collaborate to "secure a monopoly on the level and structure of taxation", with the possibility that they will use the power to maintain or raise tax burdens. To oppose this Cnossen defines the other pole in the spectrum of tax coordination as tax competition. Tax competition would be advocated from a public choice perspective as a way of restraining the growth of the public sector and promoting greater efficiency within government. Cnossen himself favours the middle ground, and defines EC tax coordination as "a process aimed at removing the tax obstacles to the establishment of a single, integrated market in such a way that Member States maintain maximum flexibility in arranging their tax system" (Cnossen, 1989, p.58). Cnossen therefore acknowledges the trade-off between decentralisation and Community-level objectives.

The presumption towards decentralisation, whether on grounds of diversity in the social, political or cultural traditions of the Members or the concerns of public choice theory, implies that a case must be made for tax policy-making at the "European" tier of government. Smith (1990) considers the factors that might influence the decision:

i) An efficiency argument stemming from *market failures* induced by separate national tax policies. In particular when taxes cause externalities or *policy spill-overs* in neighbouring states. The primary example arises when fiscal frontiers are removed but Members maintain differential tax rates. Possible consequences in terms of redistribution of tax revenue among states and the impact of cross-border shopping on the economies in frontier

80

areas are discussed in more detail in section 6. More generally Smith offers three categories of international policy spill-over:

a) When national tax policies influence private sector decisions in other Member States, for example by inducing companies to alter their location decisions or by persuading consumers to do their shopping across national borders. Smith suggests a concept of "cross-country fiscal neutrality" to be used as a yardstick for this kind of spill-over.

b) Tax policies may also cause a redistribution of tax revenue among Member States. This is particularly relevant when different states traditionally have rather different revenue requirements (reflecting the relative size of their public sectors and the balance between direct and indirect taxation). Abolition of fiscal frontiers may benefit small states, such as Luxembourg, whose *overseas* revenue is large relative to it's *domestic* revenue.

c) Thirdly, greater coordination of tax policy may lead to more effective enforcement, "preventing low-tax states becoming 'tax havens'" (Smith, 1990, p.9).

The standard solutions to this form of market failure can be considered. One solution would be bilateral negotiation and the use of side payments between individual states (the *Coasian* solution). Smith argues that in practice it would be too costly to enforce binding international agreements in this context. A second possibility is for the higher a tier of government to internalise the spill-overs through a system of financial transfers (the *Pigovian* tax/subsidy solution). In terms of EC tax policy this translates into policies like the proposal for a Community clearing house for VAT revenues. This policy creates a role for the Community tier, although Smith argues that it also blurs the responsibility for national decisions (the related argument of "enforcement asymmetry" is discussed in section 6).

ii) The second argument for assignment of tax policy to the European tier lies in the technology of tax collection. If there are economies of scale in tax administration it may be optimal to centralise the policy-making. This relates to Slemrod's (1990) case for looking at the optimal choice of tax systems, rather than simply optimal

81

tax rates. It can also be seen as an extension of the administrative case for uniformity of tax rates from the national level to the Community level. Smith (1990) cites evidence from the United States which suggests that economies of scale in tax administration may be substantial. However he expresses some doubt that the findings will necessarily carry over to the legal and linguistic diversity of the EC.

To take the EC's own view of the role of tax coordination in creating the internal market, economies of scale may also accrue to the private sector if taxes are coordinated at the Community level, border controls can be removed, and markets become less fragmented. This argument takes us into section 3.2, which discusses the criteria for judging the success of the EC's tax policy.

iii) The third possibility for spill-over arises when national tax policies, particularly on direct taxes, are used to pursue different distributional goals. The resulting tax differentials may in principle create incentives for migration between Member States. Again this provides an argument for handling distributional objectives at the highest tier. In practice Smith (1990) argues that population mobility in the EC is relatively small and that "it is likely that the labour markets of Member states will remain only weakly integrated, segmented by language barriers and cultural differences that may take many years to erode". On the other end of the spectrum this prophecy also undermines the Tiebout mechanism as a basis for tax competition. Smith argues that the low population mobility together with the small number of Members within the EC, mean that a Tiebout mechanism, under which individuals could migrate to the uncoordinated and competing tax regime that best matches their own preferences, is irrelevant.[3]

4.3.2   How to Judge the EC Proposals

If we accept that the Community does have a role to play in influencing the tax policy of its Members, the question then arises by what criteria should the success of that policy be judged? The literature on tax harmonisation suggests a variety of criteria that could be applied in a normative analysis of EC policy (see, for example, Bos and Nelson, 1988; Cnossen, 1987, 1989; Pearson and Smith, 1988).

As a starting point it is worth quoting Richard Musgrave's two "fundamental tax coordination criteria", namely tax neutrality and tax base entitlement (see, for example, Cnossen, 1987, p.6). The former requires that taxes do not distort the relative prices of domesticly produced and of imported goods, and hence "the free flow trade and factors is not distorted". Adopting tax policies that avoid distortion of trade is embodied in the Treaty of Rome (articles 95–99) and is central to the objectives of the White Paper for "creating a more favourable environment for stimulating enterprise, competition and trade" (Com(85)310). Tax base entitlement requires that property rights in tax bases are clearly established (and adhered to); these should be based on the *allegiance* or *residence* principle or the *territoriality* or *source* principle, to give a *fair entitlement* to tax revenues. A corollary of Musgrave's criteria is that less coordination is required for those tax bases that have low mobility, such as labour taxes and social security contributions.

Tax or fiscal neutrality also appears as the first item on Bos and Nelson's (1988) comprehensive list of criteria that have been used to judge the EC harmonisation plans. These criteria are fiscal neutrality, avoiding fraud, ease of administration, fiscal sovereignty, and the costs and benefits to economic subjects. To reiterate, fiscal neutrality implies that there are no tax induced trade distortions, so that the pattern of pre-tax trade is no different to post-tax trade. This concept lies at the heart of discussions of the different principles of international taxation (see section 4) and has also been used to assess the desirability of uniform rates (see section 5.3). Two practical concerns are the ease of administering the tax system and the extent to which it counteracts fraud. Bos and Nelson (1988) argue that tax reforms may be beneficial in respect to fraud either if they reduce the incentive to commit fraud or if they improve the tax authorities ability to control fraud. The issue of collection costs is one factor in the debate over uniform commodity tax rates, and also relates to the question of economies of scale in tax administration raised in the previous section. Fiscal sovereignty is a concern of all Member States. The question is whether the different social, cultural and political objectives of Member States can be reflected in a tax structure designed at the EC level, and also whether it leaves room for manoeuvre in macroeconomic stabilisation policies.

Bos and Nelson (1988) also refer to the costs and benefits to citizens of the Community. This rather general criterion can clearly be given a welfarist interpretation and expressed more specifically in terms of efficiency and equity. Among other things it means that the EC should aim to achieve an efficient allocation of resources and to avoid tax policies that distort industrial competitiveness. Pearson and Smith (1988) highlight three ways that taxes may distort competitiveness. Firstly, whether they affect industrial costs in a way that influences business's location decisions. Secondly, whether domestic tax structures can be used to favour domestic production and in doing so to create market segmentation. Thirdly, whether fiscal controls can be removed at frontiers.

4.4 PRINCIPLES OF INTERNATIONAL TAXATION

4.4.1 The Equivalence Theorem

Much of the harmonisation debate has been concerned with the need to move from the current destination system to the origin principle. Under the origin principle taxes are levied at the rate of the country of production and no "visible adjustments" (Cnossen and Shoup, 1987, p.67) are required. Under the destination principle taxes are levied at the rate of the country of consumption, and border tax adjustments are required for imported goods.

The exchange rate/tax rate equivalence theorem implies that if the origin principle is substituted for the destination principle changes in the exchange rate or domestic prices will leave the pattern of trade undisturbed. This result has been central to much of the academic debate surrounding the EC harmonisation proposals. Although, if Cnossen and Shoup (1987) are to be believed when they argue, "this tenet may be of interest to the theory of tax harmonization, it is of no relevance to the real world" (Cnossen and Shoup, 1987, p.69), the attention may have been misplaced. This raises the same issues as the origin-host debate in regulation (see page 48ff).

The crucial point is the set of assumptions required for the equivalence theorem to hold. In the harmonisation literature it seems to be rather difficult to find an all-embracing list of these conditions. The following compilation draws on Cnossen and Shoup (1987, CS), and Bos and Nelson (1988, BN) and gives some impression of the ambiguity surrounding the issue:

- perfectly flexible exchange rates and prices (CS, BN)
- exchange rates determined only by prices (BN)
- initial balance of trade (CS, BN)
- a truly comprehensive and completely uniform value-added tax (CS, BN)
- no net transfer payments, such as interest on debt, between countries (CS)
- no net flow of capital to one country (CS)
- complete immobility of factors (BN)

An additional complication arises with the existence of separate excise duties (or of different rates of VAT). This implies the need to equalize the ratios between various kinds of VAT and excise rates throughout the Community, and links to Biehl's (1988) argument that it is relative not absolute tax differentials that matter in a general equilibrium setting. Johnson and Krauss (1973) emphasise that, even in theory, this result relates to the long-run effect of the change, and the stringency of the list of conditions leads Shoup to conclude that "general application ... of the equivalence theorem had better be refrained from" (Shoup (1953) quoted in Cnossen and Shoup (1987)).

Biehl (1988) takes the argument a stage further, he argues that even if all these conditions are satisfied the equivalence theorem implies that the origin and destination principles are neutral only with respect to goods transactions. He argues that this is too partial a view. The equivalence theorem will be violated if there are international transactions that:

i) Are based on the destination principle but no border adjustments can be made. This covers "invisibles" such as tourism
ii) Cases where adjustments are made but no currency transaction is involved (and hence no impact on the exchange rate) Biehl gives the example of capital transactions
iii) A combination of i) and ii)

85

These will lead to trade distortions and Biehl argues against the destination principle as it causes more "non-goods transactions" than the CMP/TUP.

4.4.2 The Restricted Origin Principle

Harmonisation of rates or reciprocal clearing agreements are unlikely to be negotiated with all the Community's trading partners in the rest of the world. Under the restricted origin principle, introduced by Shibata (1967), members adopt the origin principle for intra-Community trade but maintain the destination principle for trade with the rest of the world (note that the destination principle is the norm under GATT rules). Using a two commodity customs union model Shibata shows that, under the restricted origin principle, different tax rates would not lead to trade distortions or to transfers of real income between countries (as a result of revenue transfers). However, the work of Whalley (1979) and Berglas (1981) shows that this result does not generalise (these models are discussed in more detail in section 5.2). More recent models, that develop Berglas's approach in which the pre-tax situation is distorted by external tariffs, are discussed in Georgakopoulos (1989, 1990a, 1990b).

4.5 UNIFORMITY VERSUS DIVERSITY

The debate over the desirability of uniform commodity taxes actually deals with two separate, but related, issues: uniformity across different commodities within a particular economy, and uniformity of a particular commodity tax rate across countries. Clearly the latter is the main concern for EC harmonisation policy, but analysis of the former also raises some relevant results.

4.5.1 Efficiency

4.5.1.1 *Optimal Tax Rules*
In terms of efficiency, the first best method for raising a fixed revenue requirement is lump sum taxation as lump sum taxes only cause income effects and not substitution effects. The literature on optimal tax rules is concerned with a second best world in which lump sum taxes/subsidies

86

are not available. Then the aim is to design a tax structure that gets closest to the first best solution. If all commodities were taxable, a uniform proportional tax would be equivalent to the first best, as all possible relative prices would remain unaltered. The difficulty arises when untaxed commodities are consumed, a uniform tax then distorts the relative prices of taxed to untaxed goods. The standard untaxed commodity is leisure (that is, only work can be taxed, not the consumer's full labour endowment). This gives the setting for the classic Ramsey-Samuelson rule which shows that, in general, uniform taxes will not be optimal.

To illustrate the cases where uniform taxes are optimal it is useful to start with the characterisation theorem provided by Sadka (1977). Sadka adopts the Diamond and Mirlees framework of a single consumer, who consumes leisure (x_0) and n consumer goods ($x_1..x_n$), with a linear production technology and perfect competition among producers, implying fixed producer prices (p). The policymaker's problem is to choose n specific tax rates (t) for the consumer goods in order to maximise consumer welfare (measured by the indirect utility function $v(q)$, where $q = p + t$), subject to a minimum revenue requirement. The tax on labour is normalised to zero (that is, $t_0 = 0$).

Sadka's theorem shows that, so long as the second order conditions are satisfied, the following statements are equivalent:

a) A uniform tax on all consumer goods (that is, $q_i = p_i/\pi$) is optimal
b) All consumer goods have the same compensated cross elasticity with respect to the wage rate.
c) Given the revenue constraint, uniform taxes maximise the supply of labour.

This theorem helps to make sense of key results from the literature on optimal second best taxation. In a 3 good economy Diamond and Mirlees (1971) show that b) is a sufficient condition for a). They also show that if labour supply is perfectly elastic, which necessarily implies c) then uniform taxes are optimal.

A crucial step in Sadka's proof that b) implies a) is to show that $s_{0k} = \beta x_k$, that is, that the Slutsky substitution term between leisure and good k is proportional to x_k. This result is also shown by Sandmo (1974). while Dixit (1975) shows that b) is a necessary condition for a). Sadka's result highlights the key role of the restrictions on individual preferences that are required to make uniform commodity taxes optimal. Atkinson and Stiglitz (1972) show that uniformity is optimal if the direct utility function is additively separable $u(x) = G(x_0) + F(x_1 ....x_n)$ and F is homothetic. Sandmo (1974) shows that this can be generalised to $u(x) = W(x_0, F(x_1 ...x_n))$ where F is homothetic which still implies $s_{0k} = \beta x$.

The importance of separability restrictions on preferences is central to Deaton's use of the cost function and distance function (Deaton (1979, 1980), and see also Besley and Jewitt (1990) for more recent developments). This approach is adopted by Kay and Keen (1987) when they discuss the specific relevance of optimal tax rules to the harmonisation of alcohol taxes. Kay and Keen adopt Deaton's formulation of the problem in terms of the distance function $d(x,u)$. They demonstrate the result that the optimal taxes for a group of goods will be uniform if and only if the distance function is implicitly separable between those commodities and any other (untaxed) commodities (such as leisure). The corresponding result in terms of the cost function is that it should be implicitly separable between leisure and other goods to justify a uniform tax on all goods, that is, $c(q,w,u) = C(w,G(q,u),u)$. Deaton's result can also be tied-in with Sadka's by noting that, with implicit separability of the cost function (and using Shephard's lemma),

$$s_{0k} = x_k (\delta G/\delta C)(\delta^2 C/\delta w \delta G) = x_k \beta$$

The intuition behind these results lies in the distinction between taxed and untaxed goods, and the fact that a uniform tax will distort the price of each of the taxed goods relative to the untaxed good, leisure, by the same proportion. As Sandmo (1987) points out, taxing the goods that are complementary with leisure provides an indirect way of taxing leisure, the separability restrictions imply that the cross-price effects, and hence the degree of complementarity, between the taxed goods and leisure are proportional to the "income effect" for that group of goods.

Using this approach, differentiation of tax rates is justified in terms of variations in relative shadow prices, where the shadow prices are given by $\delta d(x,u)/\delta x$. Kay and Keen are particularly interested to see whether optimal tax rules provide a rationale for uniformity of taxes on alcohol. They argue that "in the absence of any reason to suppose that, for instance, the shadow price of spirits relative to that of wine varies with leisure – and we can think of none – there is some presumption in favour of uniformity" (Kay and Keen, 1987, p.92).

Kay and Keen take the argument a step further when they consider the EC policy of taxing beer and spirits according to alcohol content. This leads them to reformulate the optimal tax problem in terms of characteristics (using the approach of Gorman (1956, published 1980) and Lancaster (1971)).

Characteristics (z) are assumed to be linked to market goods (x) by a fixed coefficients technology, $z = \Delta x$. Using the distance function, they show that the shadow price of a particular good is given by the weighted sum of the shadow prices of its characteristics, with weights given by the implicit value share of the characteristics. Leisure is treated as a "distinct characteristic with no other sources or uses". When the Ramsey rule is reformulated in terms of the shadow prices of characteristics, it implies that goods which are high in characteristics that are complementary with leisure will be taxed more heavily. So "for alternative forms of drink ... does indeed suggest that optimal commodity taxes will vary systematically with alcohol content, tending to be higher on stronger drinks so long as alcohol is q-complementary with leisure" (Kay and Keen, 1987, p.94). A conclusion which does seem to match the pattern of alcohol taxation in the EC.

Kay and Keen are careful to qualify this result. Firstly, they note that alcohol content in itself may not be a relevant characteristic from the consumer's point of view (although the marketing of alcohol free, low alcohol, and extra strong beers suggests that it is). Secondly, they argue that other characteristics of alcoholic drinks are relevant to the consumer's choice. In fact, if a group of goods contains only a sub-group of characteristics, and if the distance function is implicitly separable between those characteristics and leisure, the optimal commodity taxes will again be uniform for that group. Once again the presumption is in favour of taxing alcoholic drinks at the same rate.

In the case of alcohol (and tobacco) taxes, those concerned with the social and medical impact of consumption have argued that EC policy has favoured trade objectives at the expense of health objectives (see, for example, Godfrey and Powell, 1985; Powell, 1988, 1989). High taxes on "undesirable" habits, such as smoking and drinking, may reflect social policy objectives. However, these higher rates need not imply a merit good argument. Differential rates may be justified on efficiency grounds

89

if the harmful effects of alcohol and tobacco (and for that matter petrol) impose externalities. This provides a rationale for Pigovian taxes to internalise the marginal social costs (this approach is incorporated into the optimal tax framework by Sandmo (1975)).

So far the results suggest that the standard optimal tax rules would only provide an efficiency argument for uniformity under rather restrictive conditions or in the case of a narrowly defined and closely related group of goods. However as Rose (1987) points out, the results of optimal tax theory tend to be rather sensitive to the model specification that has been adopted. His response is to tailor an optimal tax model to some of the stylised features of EC institutions. In particular his model allows for guaranteed producer prices in agriculture (with Community funded stores of surpluses which make no contribution to consumers' welfare), the existence of "own resources" based on an EC VAT levied at a uniform ad valorem rate, and external tariffs on some of the goods traded with the rest of the world. His strategy is to compare an uncoordinated tax policy, in which each Member maximises the welfare of their *representative consumer* taking the tax policy of other Members as given, and a coordinated strategy in which the Community maximises a social welfare function for all Member States. Comparison of the coordinated and uncoordinated solutions does not support the optimality of uniform rates across Member States. This leads Rose to conclude that "the closer alignment of excise and value-added tax rates has no obvious claim to a social welfare optimum in the EC." (Rose, 1987, p.125).

4.5.1.2 *Welfare-improving Reforms*
It would appear that optimal tax rules provide rather limited support for uniform rates on efficiency grounds. The conditions required are rather restrictive, except perhaps in the case of closely related commodities.

In fact the EC has stressed that it does no intend to design an optimal system, but to make pragmatic improvements by approximating existing rates. In terms of normative analysis this moves us to the search for welfare-improving tax reforms. Do these theories tell us anything about the desirability of a move towards uniformity?

Two recent papers by Keen (1987, 1989) seek to answer this question. He adopts the theory of Pareto improving marginal tax reforms (see, for example, Ahmad and Stern,1984) but, like Rose, he tailors the modelling strategy to the institutions of the EC. In particular he considers the plans

90

for approximation around existing Community rates. He uses a model in which lump-sum taxes are available but in which countries still impose distortionary commodity taxes in the initial situation, either due to protectionism or "sheer perversity". To model the approximation proposals the reform is treated as a uniform proportionate convergence of domestic tax rates towards a weighted Community average. The selection of the weights is important; for the two country model the "harmonising reforms" are,

$$\left[\frac{dt}{dT} \right] = \beta \left[\begin{matrix} H - t \\ H - T \end{matrix} \right]$$

where β is a small positive scalar, t is the vector of home taxes, T is the vector of foreign taxes, and

$$H = \left[c_{qq} + C_{QQ} \right]^{-1} (c_{qq}t + C_{QQ}T)$$

where c denotes the representative consumers' cost functions (home and foreign), the q's are final prices, and subscripts denote differentiation. The choice of these particular weights ensures that world prices are not affected by the reforms; the compensated change in demand for a good in one country will be exactly offset by the compensated change in the other, so that aggregate demand remains constant.

Keen (1987) shows that, starting from an initial position of unequal rates, the harmonising reform will give a strict potential Pareto improvement. In Keen (1989) this result is strengthened by showing that the reform will lead to an actual Pareto improvement if, in the initial situation, each country has a tax structure that favours its own exports. In this case compensation between countries would not be required.

4.5.2 Neutrality

Tax neutrality, that is the avoidance of trade distortions, has been a central criterion in the evaluation of the EC's proposals. A series of theoretical papers have addressed this issue using the customs union framework. Whalley (1979) sets out to test the hypothesis that removal of trade distortions requires uniform tax rates. He uses a simple goods mobile, factors immobile general equilibrium model of international trade. The model generates two main results. Firstly, under the origin or the destination principles, uniformity is "not necessary to remove distortions of trade between integrating countries since exchange rates (or domestic price levels) can adjust to compensate for tax rate differences" (Whalley, 1979, p.214). Secondly, under the restricted origin principle, "nondistortion of trade can only occur where trade is bilaterally balanced", making uniformity irrelevant. Berglas (1981) objects to Whalley's second result. He shows that the restricted origin principle is "non-distortive", in the sense that trade flows are unaffected, so long as all countries adopt uniform rates. But even if they do adopt uniformity there will be a transfer of real income "except where each member country's trade with the rest of the world is initially balanced" (Berglas, 1981). Whalley (1981) responds by pointing out that the disagreement is basically semantic, and that in his earlier paper he adopts a unconventional definition of "trade distortion", which includes transfers of real income.

Among the more practical lessons of these papers is that they show that the claim that the origin principle is non-distorting rests on immobility of factors which, in itself, contradicts the aims of the common market. Similarly the equivalence results also rest on flexible exchange rates, which again seems inconsistent with the objectives of European monetary union.

The assumption of no factor mobility is relaxed in the more practical arguments that have been made for uniformity on the basis of companies' location decisions and their cost competitiveness. These are discussed in Smith (1988) in the context of excise duties. He argues that, under the current destination principle, excise duties on consumer goods such as alcohol and tobacco are fiscally neutral; imports pay the same duty as domestically produced goods. However this is not true of intermediate goods such as mineral oils which are purchased as inputs by industry. Concern over the impact of these duties on industrial costs leads to lower duties on diesel than on petrol.

National diversity in the structure of excise duties may also lead to market segmentation. A high ad valorem component can be used to favour low cost and quality tobacco, so-called *vertical differentiation*. While narrow definition of product categories can be used to create *horizontal differentiation,* again with the aim of favouring domestic production. Market segmentation limits the scope for industrial

92

restructuring and rationalization and hence the scope to exploit the internal market.

Along with these direct arguments for uniformity of rates, Smith (1988) also mentions the indirect arguments stemming from the abolition of frontier controls without a move to uniformity of rates. In particular the possibility that the incentive to evade single-stage excise duties, and the level of cross-border shopping will increase. These issues are dealt with in more detail below.

4.6   PROPOSALS AND COUNTER-PROPOSALS: THE ECONOMIC ARGUMENTS

4.6.1 Harmonisation versus Competition

The Commission's view is that approximation is a precondition for the Internal Market (for example, Com(85)310, Com(87)320; Guieu and Bonnet, 1987; Bos and Nelson, 1988). They argue that a single market in which there is a free-flow of goods, services, and factors requires the abolition of fiscal formalities at intra-Community frontiers. Easson (1988) neatly summarises the logic of the "Commission's position" with respect to the correct (long-run) principle of taxation: the current destination-based system requires border tax adjustments, border tax adjustments would seem to imply border controls (which are anathema to a single market without frontiers), the alternative to the destination principle is the origin principle, "ergo the Community must adopt the origin principle" (Easson, 1988). To take this argument a stage further, if the equivalence theorem for the origin and destination principles does not apply in reality, and if distortions of trade and large scale redistributions of tax revenue among Member States are to be avoided, the origin principle should be combined with "approximate" uniformity of rates. This conforms to the Commission's objectives to "secure equity between Member States and the minimum disruption in each sector" (Com(87)16), objectives which meet Musgrave's criteria of "fair entitlement" and "efficient resource mobilization".

The Commission's view has not gone unchallenged, both politically and academically. The principal opposing view questions the need for

93

harmonisation, or even "approximation", and advocates a unified system but differential rates. This would be facilitated by administrative changes that remove the need for border controls (but not fiscal controls) without requiring uniformity of rates. A key contribution is Cnossen's proposals for deferred accounting in the case of VAT (Cnossen, 1983; Cnossen and Shoup, 1987). In the UK this view has been developed most extensively in work from the Institute for Fiscal Studies (see, for example, Smith, 1988; Lee, Pearson and Smith, 1989; Pearson and Smith, 1989; Smith, 1990), and is also reflected in the UK Government's position (for example, Brooke, 1989; Jefferson Smith, 1989).

Cnossen (1989, 1990) makes the case for diversity rather than uniformity of tax rates. He argues that "far reaching tax harmonisation is neither necessary nor desirable", and presents six points in favour of diversity:

1) It is not the process of harmonisation that is significant but the end that it is intended to achieve. Cnossen argues that the Commission has not been able to give a clear definition of its objective and "if the goal can't be clearly articulated it is better left alone". This argument, which is also advanced by Kay and Keen (1987b), would seem to hold true for the rates on which Members are being asked to harmonise. These are simply pragmatic proposals based on averaging of existing rates, without clearly articulated reasons for selecting those particular levels (although recall Keen's (1987, 1989) results).

2) Legal uniformity may not imply uniformity in actual application. Cnossen quotes the Danish and Italian VAT systems to illustrate the point that taxes which are "identical on paper" may differ greatly in practice. Taxation requires effective enforcement and the method of tax administration determines the effective rate paid by each Member State's citizens.

3) Simply concentrating on the distortionary effects of taxes may be too partial. It is better to consider the overall effect of taxes and public expenditure (what Cnossen calls fiscal neutrality). This implies a second best argument that distorting tax differentials may offset public subsidies to domestic industries such as infrastructure expenditure. A variation on this point is embodied in the view that harmonisation of indirect taxes may have gone

94

far enough and is in danger of creating distortions itself if similar attention isn't paid to direct taxes, particularly corporate taxes. This view underlies many of the contributions in Gammie and Robinson (1989).

4) The fourth point is a practical consequence of the fiscal sovereignty argument. If further progress is made with monetary union (on top of the long established abolition of intra-Community tariffs) national governments will lose an extra degree of freedom in their domestic macroeconomic policymaking and the role of fiscal policy for stabilisation will be more important. On the other side of the coin, allowing countries to maintain flexibility in their tax rates may actually encourage progress towards monetary union.

5) The fifth point is an appeal to empirical evidence. Cnossen cites the evidence of other federal systems that maintain diversity in their tax systems. As he says, "no one asserts that the United States does not constitute a single, domestic market". It is worth noting that the Cockfield proposals make use of the same analogy with the US system in advocating a 5 per cent band for acceptable variation of approximated rates.

6) Returning again to the general criteria for judging the harmonisation proposals, Cnossen argues that uniformity ignores differences national preferences for particular types of tax, for the balance between direct and indirect taxes, and for the proportion of GDP devoted to the public sector. Easson (1988) chooses some revealing examples to emphasise national (merit-) preferences when he remarks, "it is not difficult to imagine the reaction, say, to an attempt in Britain to slash the tax on cigars, champagne and cognac and to introduce tax on bread, milk and baby clothes. Nor would the imposition of a tax on wines prove exactly popular in Germany or Italy" (Easson, 1988, p.250). The problem of the direct-indirect balance is raised by Guieu and Bonnet (1987) who expect that Denmark will have to make a "fundamental recasting of the structural redistribution between direct and indirect taxes" (Guieu and Bonnet, 1987, p.219). The point about differing revenue requirements of the Member states is supported by the statistics quoted in Smith (1990, Table 2, p.10). These show that tax revenues as a proportion of GDP (measured in 1986) vary

from 30.4 in Spain to 50.6 in Denmark. Smith argues that EC tax policy should respect these differences and should "seek to minimise .... distortionary effects whilst causing the least disturbance to Member States' revenue raising powers" (Smith, 1990, p.9). Smith's argument applies to both poles of coordination policy, it is clear that complete harmonisation has significant implications for revenue. But Smith argues that this problem also means that unrestricted tax competition would be undesirable. In the presence of spill-overs, tax competition may lead to a downward spiral of tax rates and hence of potential revenue. This argument forms the basis of the case for tax minima outlined in the next section.

4.6.2 Reform of VAT

The current position in the EC is that VAT is based on the destination principle and exports are zero-rated. The Cockfield proposals included the abolition of zero-rating for exports, exports would then be invoiced VAT inclusive, eliminating the need for fiscal formalities at frontiers. This brings administrative problems, each registered trader still deals with their national tax authority but "each national VAT administration would have to handle claims for input VAT credit from purchases arising in all Member States" (Smith, 1990). Also, while countries maintain different rates of VAT there would be a transfer of revenue in favour of those with higher than average rates. In fact, even if rates were uniform, those countries with an intra-Community trade surplus would still gain.

To get around these problems (and hence maintain the country of consumption as the principle for "fair entitlement" to tax revenues), the Commission proposed a computerised clearing house to reallocate revenue between members. The case for a centralised clearing mechanism also stems from a concern for the "integrity" of the system (Smith, 1990). If left to bilateral arrangements between Members one country will have "little incentive to check false VAT input claims" (Smith, 1990) and hence to guarantee the revenue entitlement of the other Member. Once again a spill-over exists, this time in tax enforcement, and the clearing-house located at the "European tier" is a way of internalising the potential problem. The clearing house proposals received a hostile political reception; and the Commission now proposes a "simplified mechanism" based on intra-Community trade balances (Bulletin of the EC, 1989).

Easson (1988) points out that in the case of multi-stage taxes like VAT a move away from the destination principle would be to the CMP/ TUP rather than the simple origin principle, with each country taxing value-added. In this case competition would not be distorted, as the domestic rate would be paid on the retail stage of production (so that *domestic* goods and imports would face the same rate). But there would be a redistribution of revenue between countries with different rates (and different tax bases due to zero-rating).

With the political reception received by many of the Cockfield proposals, much of the debate has shifted to ways of maintaining the destination principle and at the same time removing the need for fiscal controls at frontiers. The so-called *destination principle solutions* are described by Cnossen and Shoup (1987) (see also Easson, 1988) who list two categories:

i) Deferred payment schemes, such as the Postponed Accounting System (PAS) (see Cnossen, 1983), in which the border tax adjustment is shifted away from the physical border to the first taxable person

ii) Tax credit clearance schemes; in this case tax on exports is not rebated but the importer receives tax credit for the tax invoiced by the exporter. Operation of this system would require an EC clearing mechanism.

The tax credit scheme is seen as a long-run solution, while deferred payments are a "tried and proven system" (Com(85,p.43)310) used in the Benelux countries, and in the UK and Ireland before they moved back from deferral to border controls. The 1988 Lawson plan agreed to implement PAS in the UK.

All of these proposals are really aimed at the *halfway* solution of shifting fiscal formalities from the physical frontier inland. In fact the White Paper recognises this argument and responds that "a true internal, or unified, market would not require border tax adjustments, whether or not these occurred at frontier posts" (Com(85)310. Guieu and Bonnet (1987) argue that "controls carried out at borders already concern only a small percentage of intra-Community trade". They also mention the single administrative document and its potential for reducing the cost of frontier formalities. In their view it is the "market fragmentation" caused by differential rates that is the more fundamental problem for completion of a true internal market.

The proposals outlined above are concerned with the spill-over effects on Members' revenue when border controls are removed (under the destination principle with diversity in rates). They do not cover the additional spill-over effects caused by *cross-border shopping,* in other words by transactions with non-registered individuals. The main concern here is with individuals who physically travel across national frontiers. The geographic areas where cross-border shopping is most likely are the German/Danish border, the Ireland/N.Ireland border, and between the Benelux countries, France and Germany (see, for example, Owen and Dynes, 1989).

The resource costs associated with this kind of spill-over fall under two headings: the loss of revenue to the consumers' government and the deadweight loss (in terms of time and money) to consumers of making an extra effort to cross-border shop. This is a deadweight loss in the sense that the incentive to shop in this way stems purely from the tax differential. Smith and Pearson (1988) argue that these costs "fall entirely on citizens and government of the Member State levying higher tax rates than its neighbours" (Smith and Pearson, 1988, p.33) They develop this line of argument to support the case for setting tax minima rather than a Community rate or band. The rationale is that any State setting a rate above the Community minimum will bear all the costs (which they may be willing to do for national social and political objectives), while any state setting a rate below the minimum is under-cutting its neighbours and hence causing an externality. This externality justifies action at the European level.

While this argument is persuasive, it is not clear that the assertion that all costs are borne by the high rate state is true if a general equilibrium view is adopted. Substantial flows of cross border shoppers are likely to have an impact on the frontier economy of the neighbouring state, pulling-up market prices and perhaps causing other problems such as congestion.

As well as cross border shopping, international mail order also poses a problem. An example of the kind of mail-order trade that might benefit would be UK suppliers of zero-rated goods such as children's clothing. Easson (1988) recognises that cross frontier mail order is "potentially more serious" and suggests that a special scheme may be required, something that the Commission has been looking into. However he does point out that mail order adjustments do not occur at the physical frontiers and in that sense pose no problem for the elimination of border controls.

4.6.3 Reform of Excise Taxes

Excise duties are single stage taxes, levied at a single point in the chain of production. They are also charged at higher relative rates than VAT in many Member states, and the consequences for redistribution of revenue as a result of tax differentials and abolition of border controls are substantial. Gammie and Robinson (1989) suggest that "the potential revenue losses from opening the frontiers are huge" and that as a result political concerns may mean that "the goal of abolishing customs posts is dropped or deferred". The European Policy Committee predicted a loss of 11% of total tax revenue in Denmark and 5-7% in Ireland as a result of the Cockfield plan, along with increase in revenue for countries that are required to introduce duties on alcohol and tobacco such as Spain, Portugal and Greece (Smith and Pearson, 1988) . The potential gains from evasion are also likely to be greater than VAT, as is the need for control and enforcement.

To give a more detailed impression of the magnitudes involved we can turn to empirical simulations of the impact of the Cockfield proposals for expenditure patterns and revenue in the UK. Lee, Pearson, and Smith (1989) estimate a household demand system, using Deaton and Muellbauer's AIDS model, with monthly price data from the RPI and a pooled cross-section of the Family Expenditure Survey from 1970 to 1984. They use the estimated system to carry out a simulation based on a sample of 7000 households from the 1984 FES (for a similar study of Greece see Nikolaou (1990)). They consider the full range of the Cockfield proposals: abolition of zero-rating means that goods such as food, household energy, books and newspapers are charged at the reduced rate of 4%, while children's clothing, which is not in the base for the EC reduced rate band, is charged at the standard rate. Changes in excise duties are taken from UK Government predictions; these anticipated that the tax on a bottle of spirits would fall by £2.30, the tax on a bottle of wine would fall by 70p, the average tax on the price of 20 cigarettes would fall by 32p, and that petrol duty would rise by 20p per gallon.

Among Lee, Pearson and Smith's forecasts the most dramatic effects are on alcohol. Consumption of all alcoholic drinks is predicted to increase by 12% in value terms and 39% in volume terms, while government revenue from alcohol is predicted to fall by £1.9bn. The overall effect of the proposed changes in VAT and excise duties is a predicted £0.8bn net increase in revenue.

Along with substantial variation in the rates charged and, to some extent, the goods covered the administration and control of excises duties also varies across Member States. Smith (1988) lists two approaches to excises administration:

i) *Close supervision,* in which tax authorities monitor the production and movement of dutiable merchandise until the moment the duty is paid, an example is the UK system of bonded warehouses.
ii) *Marking.* Many countries, for example the Benelux nations, Denmark, W.Germany, and Greece, use physical stamps or "banderoles" to indicate whether duty has been paid.

Smith points out that current intra-Community trade is free of these controls and if fiscal frontiers are removed the current systems, and particularly close supervision, will become unworkable. The official view is summed up by Guieu and Bonnet, "approximation of rates is, in the opinion of the Commission, an indispensable precondition for the abolition of frontier controls" (Guieu and Bonnet, 1989, p.214). However Smith (1988) argues that "elimination of duty differentials between Member States is not essential for the completion of the Internal Market". Instead he proposes an administrative solution to avoid the unwanted redistribution of revenue among the members. As with VAT, this theme of altering the tax mechanism to permit the removal of border controls has found favour with the UK authorities. For example, the Deputy Chairman of HM Customs and Excise, Peter Jefferson Smith asks; "how can we change the mechanics of tax collection so that they will still work after tax frontiers have been abolished?" (Jefferson Smith, 1989). The importance of this perspective is that it is seen as an alternative to harmonisation of rates as the necessary condition for abolition of frontiers. The UK Government presents this as an attempt to recast the problem as "technical" rather than "political" (Brooke, 1989; Jefferson Smith, 1989)

100

To cope with the problem of revenue spill-overs a system of linked bonded warehouses has been proposed. This would allow goods to travel across borders while remaining in bond (duty would only be paid when the goods leave bond, avoiding border adjustments). The Commission argues that the incentive for firms to delay payment of duty until as close to the point of sale as possible mean that linked warehouses would lead to the desired allocation of revenue. Smith (1988) casts some doubt on this hope, he points out that economies of scale in distribution may outweigh the cash-flow incentives, leading large firms to centralise their warehousing (and presumably leading to a reallocation of revenues to the geographic heart of the Community). This argument is supported by Wolfgang Ritter, of BASF and the Confederation of German Industry, who argues that a system of linked warehouses "are an advantage to companies in terms of liquidity but has a limiting effect on freedom of the transport of goods, which can be a great hindrance in the rationalisation of the lines of distribution in particular goods for mass consumption" (Ritter, 1989, p.79).

Smith (1988) considers the alternative policy of marking for country of consumption to prevent the movement of duty paid goods across frontiers, and Gammie and Robinson (1989) emphasise that these banderoles would be used to control commercial transactions, which would be outlawed, without preventing personal importing. Jefferson Smith (1989) talks about a similar proposal for a system based on accompanying documents. However, it is not clear from these proposals exactly how the process of marking and revenue collection would be administered. It could be done in the country of production, but that would require compensating revenue transfers to ensure fair entitlement. Or it could be combined with system of linked warehouses. The latter seems more expensive, but it creates the right incentives for enforcement as the authority administering the marking would be entitled to the revenue.

One problem with marking for country of consumption is that it may cause some loss in potential market integration. Lee, Pearson and Smith (1988) suggest larger duty zones and argue that three zones could be created from the current membership of the Community with "little disturbance to existing patterns". This view is echoed in Jenkins (1989) who points to the clear differential in duty levels between the North and the South of the Community. He argues that "it should be possible to

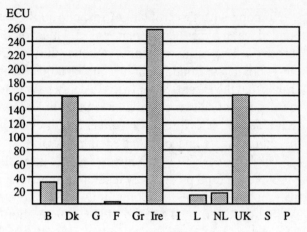

Figure 4.2a
Excise rates
per HL still wine,
1989

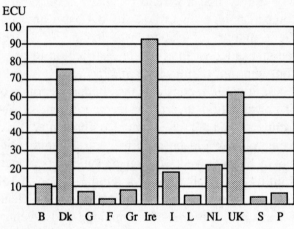

Figure 4.2b
Excise rates
per HL average
beer, 1989

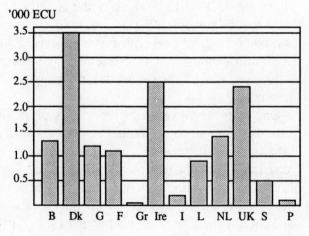

Figure 4.2c
Excise rates
per HL pure spirits,
1989

Source: COM (89) 551

reach a pragmatic agreement whereby differences are kept within well defined limits for neighbouring states, but allowed to remain somewhat larger as between states whose frontiers are distant from each other."

Another problem with marking is the need for control and enforcement to "prevent the establishment of a commercial trade in dutiable goods". Gammie and Robinson (1989) suggest that a system of random checks would be needed. However they also recognise that "both the costs of these checks and the amount of evasion would probably be greater than under the existing system of frontier controls" (Gammie and Robinson, 1989, p.5). To keep the problem of frontier controls and possible administrative alternatives in perspective they emphasise that the bulk of intra-Community trade in dutiable goods is movement of freight rather than personal trade and they therefore feel confident to conclude that "a stamp scheme for dealing with excise duties will actually achieve the substance of 1992 for all industries except alcohol and tobacco, and the associated gains will more than offset any additional policing costs".

With respect to tobacco, Cnossen (1989) suggests that the EC does not face too great a problem. He notes that total effective rates of ad valorem tax (including VAT) and specific duty are actually quite similar for most Member States. In 1989 the range was 67–75%, except for Denmark with an effective rate of 86%. Of course this masks the wide variation in the balance of ad valorem and specific rates, an issue discussed in more detail in section 6.4. In the case of alcohol the Community is still a long way from effective approximation, the continuing differences are illustrated by Figure 4.2.

The administrative changes may help to protect the allocation of revenue but, as with VAT, differential rates may induce other spillover effects such as cross-border shopping and international mail order. Once again there is the possibility that tax competition among neighbouring states may lead to undercutting and a downward spiral in rates. As with VAT the IFS response is to advocate tax minima; minimum rates designed to put a floor on the competitive spiral. They argue that countries setting rates above the minima will bear the costs of the decision themselves and that are therefore "no grounds for Community control over their decision" (Smith, 1988). They also predict that in the longer term there may be a convergence in rates as a response to the spill-overs. The tax minima approach has made its way into the latest Commission proposals on excise taxes (see section 2).

Marking and linked warehousing are administrative changes concerned with commercial trade. As regards personal trade, Mme Scrivener has proposed increases in travellers allowances by 1992 (see, for example, Gammie and Robinson, 1989). Jefferson Smith (1989) goes further and argues that no quantity or value limit should be imposed on VAT-able goods. Although he recognises that "disparities of excise rates and considerations of health are such that we doubt if the limits can be abolished entirely". The UK Government also argues that border controls will still be required for the prevention of drug smuggling and terrorism.

Other issues still remain unresolved in the area of excise duties. Despite the framework directive in 1972, there is still considerable diversity in the excise tax base among Member States. As evidence of the inertia in EC progress towards harmonisation of excise taxes Jefferson Smith (1989) notes that "there has not even been acceptance that the excises on goods should be the classical trio of tobacco, alcohol and oil". Ritter (1989) describes the lack of approval for simultaneous abolition of duties on coffee, tea, sugar, salt, and lighting equipment in the Federal Republic, and is relieved to say that "luckily we have still been protected from the Commission's proposal for a wine tax" (Ritter, 1989, p.78). Other examples include Italy where there also is duty on sugar, coffee, salt and matches.

Finally, a radical solution to the problems caused by diverse and often high excise rates is to do away with them entirely. Easson (1988) considers the idea of incorporating traditional excise taxes into the VAT system, and charging higher rates where appropriate. In support of this approach he argues that "there is after all, no intrinsic merit in taxing wine on the basis of alcoholic content or beer on the number of worts, rather than taxing these products ad valorem" (Easson, 1988, p.259). This view is in stark contrast to the economic analysis described below.

4.6.4 Specific versus Ad Valorem Taxes

Much of the EC discussion of tobacco tax harmonisation has concerned the appropriate balance between the specific and ad valorem components of cigarette taxes. The continuing diversity in this balance is illustrated by Figure 4.3, which shows the clear *North-South* divide on this issue.

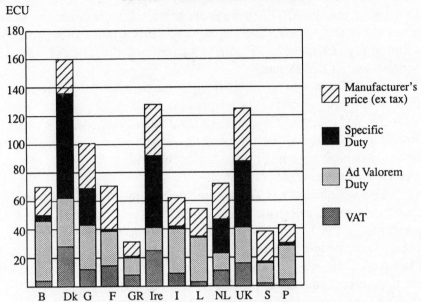

Figure 4.3a
Structure of tobacco taxes: 1.04.89

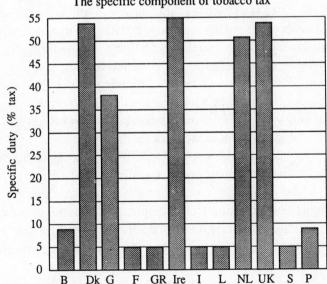

Figure 4.3b
The specific component of tobacco tax

Source: COM(89)551

Figure 4.3.a) shows the breakdown of the typical price of cigarettes into the manufacturer's price (PR), the specific duty (TAX), the ad valorem duty (AV), and the VAT. Among other things, this illustrates the point made above that the effective tax rates are fairly similar throughout the Community. In contrast, Figure 4.3.b) shows the diversity in the composition of the tax rate.

In the UK, prior to 1973, tax liability for the specific component of cigarette taxes depended on the weight of tobacco in the cigarette. After a transitional phase, the EC system was adopted in 1978 (see, for example, Brown and Jackson, 1990), this consists of an ad valorem element based on the recommended retail price (in addition to VAT), and a specific element based on number of cigarettes

In line with Barzel's (1976) argument about the market's response to untaxed characteristics, the change lead to a shift towards king size cigarettes in the UK market. Under the EC system tobacco content became an untaxed characteristic, and the result provides "an excellent example of the way in which taxes can influence the behaviour of manufacturers and customers" (Brown and Jackson, 1990, p.504).

The analytical issues raised by the balance between ad valorem and specific taxes have been explored in a series of papers by Kay and Keen (1983, 1987a, 1987b), building on the earlier work of Bishop (1968) and Barzel (1976). They start with the "standard case" of perfect competition and exogenous product quality and show that the two methods of taxation are "essentially equivalent", in the sense that either method can be used to generate the same equilibrium quantity and level of tax revenue, and that the choice is simply a "matter of administrative convenience".

Once product quality and variety are endogenous the equivalence of ad valorem and specific taxes breaks down. Kay and Keen look at the implications of this phenomenon for both tax revenue and welfare maximisation. In Kay and Keen (1987a) they start by considering a multiplicative specification of product quality, qx, where q is the quality parameter. In the limit, a specific tax makes no contribution to revenue due to product concentration (for example, pure alcohol could be sold, for the consumer to dilute to the desired strength). The revenue maximising ad valorem rate is given by the inverse of the price elasticity of demand.

To avoid product concentration Kay and Keen also consider an additive specification, where the "full price" of the good is, $p + H(q)$, where H is strictly convex. In this case revenue maximisation implies a wholly specific tax, again set equal to the inverse of the price elasticity when expressed as a proportional rate. In this case the ad valorem tax gives manufacturers an incentive to reduce product quality. From a welfare point of view the optimal ad valorem rate is also zero.

This rather strong result is qualified by two cases where non-zero ad valorem taxes may be optimal. In Kay and Keen (1983) they use a Salop-style model of product variety and show that the ad valorem rate can be used to achieve the desired degree of variety. In Kay and Keen (1987b) they show that an ad valorem rate may also have a role if distributional concerns are relevant as well as efficiency. If the consumption of poorer quality products is correlated with lower incomes, ad valorem taxes will be more progressive than specific taxes. Kay and Keen doubt the relevance of this last point for EC policy and point out that other aspects of the tax-benefit system are likely to be more effective in achieving distributional goals.

These analytical arguments are translated into a policy proposal by Smith (1988) who favours removing Member States discretion in setting the ad valorem element of tobacco duty. This would of course be a consequence of the EC approximation proposal for a target band of 54–56%.

4.7 CONCLUSION

This chapter has shown that economic concepts and analysis have played a useful role in the debate over European tax harmonisation. A debate that is still to be settled. Advocates of harmonisation, must recognise that harmonisation, particularly of excise duties, will impose substantial costs on Member States (whatever the potential benefits). As a result these proposals are likely to be dogged by continued political inertia. They must also recognise that their case suffers the weakness of lacking a clearly justified objective for the levels at which rates should be harmonised.

The advocates of continued diversity in Community tax rates have built an elaborate case for destination principle solutions which would remove the need for physical controls at frontiers; although more thought should be given to the practical details of implementing schemes such as the marking of dutiable goods. However these proposals do not eliminate the need for fiscal formalities of some kind, and more analysis needs to be devoted to the charge that this will cause fragmentation and will therefore hinder the full potential of the single market.

APPENDIX

Key Events in the Development of EC Tax Policy.

1957	Treaty of Rome. Articles 95–99 deal with harmonisation of structure and rates of indirect taxes.
1962	Neumark Report. Proposals: i) Introduce the origin principle, ii) Replace all turnover taxes with VAT
1967	Action Programme. First of series of VAT directives: Neumark proposals implemented. VAT levied on a common basis to replace turnover taxes.
1968	Customs duties on intra-Community trade removed.
1970	EC *own resources* established (based on 1% of VAT).
1972	First directive on Excise Duties. Framework directive: established list of five dutiable commodities; beer, wine, spirits, tobacco, and mineral oils. Directive on the balance of specific and ad valorem components of cigarette taxes approved by the Council.
1975	Further Action Programme on VAT.
1977	Sixth VAT Directive. Common VAT base, allowing temporary derogations (that is, for zero-rated goods)
1978	Series of European Court cases to reduce protectionism in alcohol market.
1982	Fourteenth VAT Directive. To introduce "postponed accounting" (withdrawn 1987). Proposal for computerised clearing house.
1984	UK reduces duty on wine to comply with European Court ruling.
1985	White Paper. Harmonisation an essential and integral part of internal market proposals.
1986	Delors modification of own resources, VAT becomes 1.4%, and GNP-based contribution introduced.
1987	Cockfield Plan. Commission's *approximation* proposals: – abolition of border controls by 1992 – two VAT bands: standard 14–20%, reduced rate 4–9% – clearing house for inter-country balances – EC wide duty on alcohol, tobacco and mineral oils UK threaten veto in Council of Ministers on zero-rating issue.

1988	Interim Report of EC Economic and Monetary Committee: seeks compromise between Cockfield and "market forces" view.
	Metten Proposals. Two VAT bands, zero–6/9% (accommodates zero-rating), 16–22% (accommodates Denmark's 22%)
	Lawson Plan. Put forward at meeting of EC Finance Ministers in Crete:
	– gradual elimination of restriction on cross–border shopping
	– retention of different excise rates on alcohol and tobacco, citing health arguments
	– willing to accept postponed accounting system in UK
	– emphasis on market forces
	Metten proposals approved by European Parliament's Committee on Fiscal Approximation as amendment to Cockfield plan.
1989	Lord Cockfield succeeded by Mme Christiane Scrivener as Commissioner with prime responsibility for tax issues. VAT proposals: single floor for standard rate, band of 4–9% for reduced rate. Retention of zero-rating for a small number of products under "certain conditions".
	Clearing house proposal replaced by simplified mechanism based on intra-Community trade balances.
	Latest proposals for excise rates on tobacco, alcohol, and mineral oils. Presented both short-term minima and longer term target rates or bands.

NOTES

1. An earlier version of this chapter was presented at a conference, *La Riqualificazione dell'Intervento Pubblico nell'Europa del 1992*, Panarea, 28 May – 1 June 1990. I am grateful to participants at that meeting and to Theo Georgakopoulos, David Gowland, and Theo Hitris for their comments.
2. See, for example, Musgrave, 1987; Devereux and Pearson, 1989, 1990; Pearson, 1989; Cnossen, 1990; Isard, 1990; Sinn, 1990; Sorenson, 1990.
3. For an alternative view, that predicts dire consequences for the insurance role of welfare states within the EC, see Sinn (1990).

REFERENCES

Ahmad, E. and Stern, N., (1984), "The Theory of Reform and Indian Indirect Taxes", *Journal of Public Economics*, 25: 259–298.

Atkinson, A.B. and Stiglitz, J.E., (1972), "The Structure of Indirect Taxation and Economic Efficiency", *Journal of Public Economics*, 1: 97–119.

Atkinson, A.B. and Stiglitz, J.E., (1980), *Lectures on Public Economics*, McGraw Hill.

Baker, P. and McKay S., (1990), *The Structure of Alcohol Taxes: A Hangover from the Past?*, IFS Commentary No.21.

Barzel, Y., (1976), "An Alternative Approach to the Analysis of Taxation", *Journal of Political Economy,* 84: 1177–1197.

Berglas, E., (1981), "Harmonization of Commodity Taxes. Destination, Origin and Restricted Origin Principles", *Journal of Public Economics,* 16: 377–387.

Besley, T. and Jewitt, I., (1990), "Uniform Taxation and Consumer Preferences", University of Bristol, Discussion Paper 90/259.

Bieber, R., Dehousse, R. and Pinder, J., (1988), *1992: One European Market?,* Nomos Verlagsgellschaft for The European Policy Unit at the European University Institute.

Biehl, D., (1988), "On Maximal Versus Optimal Tax Harmonization", in, Bieber, R., Dehousse, R. and Pinder, J., eds., *1992: One European Market?,* Nomos Verlagsgellschaft for The European Policy Unit at the European University Institute.

Bishop, R.L., (1968), "The Effects of Specific and Ad Valorem Taxes", *Quarterly Journal of Economics,* 82: 198–218.

Bos, M. and Nelson, H., (1988), "Indirect Taxation and Completion of the Internal Market of the EC", *Journal of Common Market Studies,* XXVII: 27–44.

Brooke, P., (1989), "The Government's Approach to the Community: Some Myths Dispelled", in, Gammie, M. and Robinson, B., eds., *Beyond 1992: A European Tax System,* Proceedings of the Fourth IFS Residential Conference, IFS Commentary No.13.

Brown, C.V. and Jackson, P.M., (1990), *Public Sector Economics,* Blackwell.

Bull.EC., (5–89), "Approximation of Indirect Taxation", *Bulletin of the European Community,* No.5, Brussels.

Bull.EC., (11–89), "Removal of Tax Frontiers", *Bulletin of the European Community,* No.5, Brussels.

Cnossen, S., (1983), "Harmonization of Indirect Taxes in the EEC", *British Tax Review,* 4: 232–253

Cnossen, S., (1987), *Tax Coordination in the European Community,* Kluwer.

Cnossen, S. and Shoup, C.S., (1987), "Coordination of Value-Added Taxes", in Cnossen, S., ed., *Tax Coordination in the EC,* Kluwer.

Cnossen, S., (1989), "How Much Tax Harmonisation in the European Community?", in, Gammie, M. and Robinson, B., eds., *Beyond 1992: A European Tax System,* Proceedings of the Fourth IFS Residential Conference, IFS Commentary No.13.

Cnossen, S., (1990), "The Case for Tax Diversity in the European Community", *European Economic Review,* 34: 471–479.

COM(85)310, (1985), *Completing the Internal Market,* Brussels.

COM(87)320, (1987), *Completion of the Internal Market: Approximation of Indirect Tax Rates and Harmonisation of Indirect Tax Structure. Global Communication from the Commission,* Brussels.

COM(89)525, (1989), *Amended Proposal for a Council Directive on the Approximation of Taxes on Cigarettes and on Manufactured Tobacco other than Cigarettes,* Brussels.

COM(89)526, (1989), *Amended Proposal for a Council Directive on the Approximation of the Rates of Excise Duty on Mineral Oils,* Brussels.

110

COM(89)527, (1989), *Amended Proposal for a Council Directive on the Approximation of Rates of Excise Duty on Alcoholic Beverages and the Alcohol Contained in Other Products*, Brussels.

COM(89)551, (1989), *New Commission Approach to Excise Duty Rates*, Brussels.

Curwen, P., (1990), *Understanding the UK Economy*, MacMillan.

Deaton, A.S., (1979), "The Distance Function in Consumer Behaviour with Applications to Index Numbers and Optimal taxation", *Review of Economic Studies*, 46: 391–406.

Deaton, A.S., (1981), "Optimal Taxes and the Structure of Preferences", *Econometrica*, 49: 1245–1260.

Dennis, G., (1981), "The Harmonisation of Fiscal Systems", in Twitchett, C.C., ed., *Harmonisation in the EEC*, MacMillan.

Devereux, M. and Pearson, M., (1989), *Corporate Tax Harmonisation and Economic Efficiency*, IFS Report Series No.35.

Devereux, M. and Pearson M., (1990), "Harmonising Corporate Taxes in Europe", *Fiscal Studies*, 11: 21–35.

Diamond, P.A. and Mirlees, J.A., (1971), "Optimal Taxation and Public Production: I and II", *American Economic Review*, 61: 8–27 and 261–278.

Dixit, A., (1975), "Welfare Effects of Tax and Price Changes", *Journal of Public Economics*, 4: 103–123.

Easson, A.J., (1988), "The Elimination of Fiscal Frontiers", in,Bieber, R., Dehousse, R. and Pinder, J., eds., *1992: One European Market?*, Nomos Verlagsgellschaft for The European Policy Unit at the European University Institute.

Gammie, M. and Robinson, B., (1989), *Beyond 1992: A European Tax System*, Proceedings of the Fourth IFS Residential Conference, IFS Commentary No.13.

Georgakopoulos, T.A., (1989), "Harmonisation of Commodity Taxes. The Restricted Origin Principle – Comment", *Journal of Public Economics*, 39: 137–139.

Georgakopoulos, T.A., (1990a), "Harmonisation of Non-general Product Taxes: The Restricted Origin Principle", mimeo, Athens University of Economics and Business.

Georgakopoulos, T.A., (1990b), "Trade Deflection, Trade Distortions and Pareto Inefficiencies under the Restricted Origin Principle", mimeo, Athens University of Economics and Business.

Godfrey, C. and Powell, M., (1985), "Alcohol and Tobacco Taxation: Barriers to a Public Health Perspective", *The Quarterly Journal of Social Affairs*, 1: 329–353.

Gorman, W.M., (1980), "A Possible Procedure for Analysing Quality Differentials in the Egg Market", *Review of Economic Studies*, XLVII, 893–906.

Guieu, P. and Bonnet, C., (1987), "Completion of the Internal Market and Indirect Taxation", *Journal of Common Market Studies*, XXV: 209–222.

Harrop, J., (1989), *The Political Economy of the Integration in the European Community*, Edward Elgar.

Helm, D. and Smith, S., (1989), "Economic Integration and the Role of the European Community", *Oxford Review of Economic Policy*, 5.

Isard, P., (1990), "Corporate Tax Harmonization and European Monetary Integration", *Kyklos,* 43: 3–24.

Jefferson Smith, P., (1989), "Proposals to Date, and Aims for 1992", in, Gammie, M. and Robinson, B., eds., *Beyond 1992: A European Tax System,* Proceedings of the Fourth IFS Residential Conference, IFS Commentary No.13.

Jenkins, C., (1989), "Taxation and the Single Market", *EIU European Trends,* 2: 79–86.

Johnson, H.G. and Krauss, M.B., (1973), "Border Taxes, Border Tax Adjustments, Comparative Advantage, and the Balance of Payments", in Krauss, M.R., ed., *The Economics of Integration,* Allen and Unwin.

Kay, J.A. and Keen, M.J., (1983), "How Should Commodities be Taxed? Market Structure, Product Heterogeneity and the Optimal Structure of Commodity Taxes", *European Economic Review,* 23: 339–358.

Kay, J. and Keen, M., (1987a), "Commodity Taxation for Maximum Revenue", *Public Finance Quarterly,* 15: 371–385.

Kay, J. and Keen, M., (1987b), "Alcohol and Tobacco Taxes: Criteria for Harmonisation", in Cnossen, S., ed., *Tax Coordination in the EC, Kluwer.*

Keen, M., (1987), "Welfare Effects of Commodity Tax Harmonisation", *Journal of Public Economics,* 33: 107–114.

Keen, M., (1989), "Pareto-improving Indirect Tax Harmonisation", *European Economic Review,* 33: 1–12.

Lancaster, K., (1971), *Consumer Demand. A New Approach,* Columbia University Press.

Lee, C., Pearson, M., and Smith, S., (1989), "Fiscal Harmonisation: An Analysis of the European Commisssion's Proposals" IFS Report R28.

Musgrave, P.B., (1987), "Interjurisdictional Coordination of Taxes on Capital Income", in Cnossen, S., ed., *Tax Coordination in the EC,* Kluwer.

Nikolaou, A., (1990), "Harmonisation of Tobacco and Alcohol Taxes in the EEC and the Welfare of Greek Consumers", Birkbeck College, Discussion Papers in Economics 4/90.

Owen, R. and Dynes, M., (1989), *The Times Guide to 1992. Britain in a Europe without Frontiers,* Times Books.

Pearson, M. and Smith, S., (1989), "1992: Issues in Indirect Taxation", *Fiscal Studies,* 9: 25–35.

Powell, M., (1988), "Data Note – 15. Alcohol and Tobacco Tax in the European Community", *British Journal of Addiction,* 83: 971–978.

Powell, M., (1989), "Tax Harmonisation in the European Community" in Robinson, R., Maynard, A., and Chester, R., (eds.), *Controlling Legal Addictions,* MacMillan.

Rose, M., (1987), "Optimal Tax Perspective on Tax Coordination", in Cnossen, S., ed., *Tax Coordination in the EC,* Kluwer.

Sadka, E., (1977), "A Theorem on Uniform Taxation", *Journal of Public Economics,* 7: 387–391.

Sandmo, A., (1974), "A Note on the Structure of Indirect Taxation", *American Economic Review,* 64: 701–706.

112

Sandmo, A., (1975), "Optimal Taxation in the Presence of Externalities", *Swedish Journal of Economics*, 77: 86–98.

Sandmo, A., (1987), "A Reinterpretation of Elasticity Formulae in Optimum Tax Theory", *Economica*, 54: 89–96.

Shibata, H., (1967), "The Theory of Economic Unions: A Comparative Analysis of Customs Unions, Free Trade Areas and Tax Unions", in Shoup, C.S., ed., *Fiscal Harmonisation in Common Markets*, Columbia University Press.

Sinn, H-W., (1990), "Tax Harmonization and Tax Competition in Europe", *European Economic Review*, 34: 489–504.

Slemrod, J., (1990), "Optimal Taxation and Optimal Tax Systems", *Journal of Economic Perspectives*, 4: 157–178.

Smith, S., (1988), "Excise Duties and the Internal Market", *Journal of Common Market Studies*, XXVII: 147–159.

Smith, S., (1990), "The European Community's Priorities in Tax Policy", IFS Working Paper No. W90/2.

Sorenson, P.B., (1990), "Tax Harmonization in the European Community: Problems and Prospects", Bank of Finland Discussion Papers 3/90.

Whalley, J., (1976), "Some General Equilibrium Analysis Applied to Fiscal Harmonization in the European Community", *European Economic Review*, 8: 291–312.

Whalley, J., (1979), "Uniform Domestic Tax Rates, Trade Distortions and Economic Integration", *Journal of Public Economics*, 11: 213–221.

Whalley, J., (1981), "Border Adjustments and Tax Harmonization: Comment on Berglas", *Journal of Public Economics*, 16: 389–390.

5 Public purchasing

Keith Hartley

5.1 INTRODUCTION: THE POLICY ISSUES[1]

Governments are major buyers of goods and services. Public procurement embraces all aspects of public sector purchasing. At one extreme, relatively simple and standard items are purchased "off-the-shelf", such as paper clips, batteries, motor cars and office equipment. At the other extreme, more complex projects are bought such as large suspension bridges, telecommunications and transport systems, nuclear power stations and space rockets. In some cases, projects require a major advance in technology and have to be designed and built to specific government requirements. Defence equipment is a good example, where new combat aircraft, guided missiles, tanks and warships are built to the requirements of a nation's armed forces.

Within the EC, there are major differences in the size and structure of the public sector and in the organisation of public procurement. For example, privatisation means that procurement decisions are transferred from the public to the private sector, where commercial and profitability criteria will determine choices. Similarly, nations differ in the extent to which public procurement is centralised or decentralised. In some cases, purchasing is undertaken locally rather than nationally, or a single government department might purchase supplies for all other departments. There are examples (for example, the UK National Health

Service) where the appearance of a single buyer is deceptive and in reality there are a variety of procurement policies at the national, regional and local levels. The EC also has substantial experience of public sector projects which have been undertaken on a collaborative basis involving a number of nations (for example, aerospace projects; ESPRIT; European Space Agency). Such a diversity of experience in the EC raises two policy-relevant questions. First, what is the policy problem? Second, what is the contribution of economic analysis in evaluating EC policy on public procurement? The emphasis of the chapter will be on general economic principles rather than a detailed descriptive account of public procurement in each EC member state. Consideration will be given to the economic logic of EC procurement policy and to the various ways in which national governments and firm might seek to thwart EC rules.

5.2 THE POLICY PROBLEM

Government procurement policy favouring national suppliers forms one of the barriers to the successful completion of the Internal Market by 1992. Public procurement in the EC in 1989 amounted to ECU 592 billion equivalent to some 15% of the Community's GDP. Within this total, EC formal purchasing rules apply to between ECU 260–380 billion or between 7% and 10% of Community GDP (EC 1989 a,b). Public purchasing is particularly concentrated on building and civil engineering, energy products (for example, electricity generation, oil), telecommunications, transport equipment and business services. However, only a small proportion of public sector contracts are awarded to companies from other EC nations. An indication of protectionism in public procurement markets is reflected in the fact that the level of imports for public contracts is considerably lower than the level of imports for EC economies. In 1987, a survey of five states (Belgium, France, Germany, Italy, UK) found that, typically, imports represented under 2% of public purchasing compared with 22% at the economy level (EC 1989, a, p.12).

It is believed that liberalising or opening-up public procurement markets will lead to substantial savings, estimated at ECU 17.2 billion or 0.5% of Community GDP over the medium to long-term. In the process, almost 400,000 new jobs will be created (Cecchini 1988; EC 1989 b).

115

The savings from more efficient public procurement will come from three sources. First, from opening national markets enabling public agencies to purchase from the cheapest suppliers (the static trade effect). Second, from increased competition as domestic firms reduce prices to compete with foreign rivals entering previously protected national markets (the competition effect). Third, from scale effects as, in the long-run, industries are rationalised and re-structured enabling the surviving firms to achieve economies of scale (the restructuring effect: Cecchini 1988).

The three sources of cost savings are shown in Figure 5.1. Buying from the cheapest supplier means access to the lowest-cost producers as shown by the reduction in unit costs from C_1 to C_0 for output Q_1 in Figure 5.1. At the same time, greater competition will lead to reduced profit margins and hence lower prices (prices fall from P_2 to P_1 and profit margins from π_1 to π_0). Finally, exploitation of scale economies will mean further reductions in unit costs and prices as output increases from Q_1 to Q_2 on the long-run cost curve C_0.

Figure 5.1
Cost and price effects

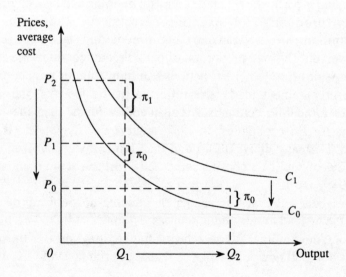

116

Table 5.1
Opening-up public procurement

		ECUs billions *(1989 prices)*
I	Savings from:	
	(i) Buying from cheapest suppliers	5.5
	(ii) Competitive pressure on prices	2.8
	(iii) Scale effects	8.9
	Total savings	17.2
II	Increase in Community GDP	+ 0.5%
III	Increase in employment	+ 350,000
IV	Additional savings from opening-up defence equipment markets (approx)	5.0

Source: EC 1989b.

The relative contribution of the trade, competition and scale effects to the estimated cost savings of some ECU 17 billion is shown in Table 5.1. The broad aggregates do, however, conceal substantial variations in the size of savings available in different EC public procurement markets. For example, the price savings from open competition (that is, trade and competition effects) have been estimated at 40–50% for pharmaceuticals in the UK and Germany; 60–70% for telephone switching equipment in Belgium and Germany; and about 10% for motor vehicles in Italy and the UK. For some products such as fluorescent tubes, cement and school desks, there are no potential savings available (Cecchini 1988, p.20). Elsewhere, in sectors where firms are too small to compete internationally, further savings are available from mergers leading to a smaller number of EC firms able to exploit economies of scale. Examples include boilers, turbine generators, electric locomotives and public exchange switching equipment where reductions in unit costs of 12–20% and more are possible (Cecchini 1988, p.22). In general, the size of cost savings available from opening-up EC public procurement will depend on the degree of monopoly or competition in national markets and the extent to which national suppliers are exploiting scale economies (see Figure 5.1). There are also likely to be indirect, difficult to quantify, benefits through lower prices for private sector buyers and the dynamic effects of greater competition on innovation, investment and growth (Catinat, 1989). Further benefits are available from opening-up EC defence equipment markets which might bring the total savings to over ECU 22 billion (1989 prices: EC 1989b, p.5). These savings from liberalising public procurement need to be assessed against the potential gains for the EC resulting from the completion of the internal market estimated at over ECU 200 billion (1988 prices: Cecchini, 1988, p.84).

5.3 POT OF GOLD ECONOMICS: A MISSED OPPORTUNITY

If the savings from opening-up public procurement markets are so large (a pot of gold), why have the EC nations apparently failed to exploit such obvious opportunities for making themselves better off? Three explanations can be suggested:

(i)   The cost savings are not as great as estimated;
(ii) The existing arrangements are optimal so that change is not worthwhile;
(iii) Public procurement markets are failing to work properly.

Estimated savings depend upon a variety of assumptions about unit costs, pricing behaviour and market structure, all of which need to be specified in order to appreciate the limitations of any model used to estimate the benefits of liberalising EC public procurement. Assumptions have to be made about pricing policy, the internal efficiency of firms, the absence of diseconomies of scale and the adjustment costs involved in re-allocating to other sectors the resources from firms and regions losing public sector contracts. For example, the model in Figure 5.1 assumed that prices are based on average costs, including a profit margin. However, firms might not reduce prices by the full extent of any cost reductions, so affecting the distribution of gains between public buyers and suppliers. Here, much will depend on the extent to which public procurement markets are contestable. Without the threat of entry, the price of efficient scale might be monopoly leading to X-inefficiency and

118

"excessive" profits. It is also possible that a major expansion of firm size beyond existing experience levels might encounter managerial diseconomies. Moreover, if EC production is rationalised and concentrated in a few localised plants, there could be increased transaction costs for public buyers as they face the possibility of higher transport and distribution costs and the possible additional costs of "doing business" with foreign rather than domestic companies. Any such additional costs will reduce the estimated savings from opening-up public procurement markets.

Focusing on the cost savings from liberalising public procurement ignores the benefits to consumers which result from purchasing products which more closely reflect their different and varied tastes and preferences. If there are believed to be substantial benefits from protected public procurement and if the savings from liberalisation are not as great as estimated, the incentive to change will be considerably reduced. Clearly, public purchasing from national firms can be rationalised and justified in terms of offering employment, regional, technological, balance of payments and strategic benefits. However, public procurement is different from private markets in that procurement officials purchase collectively on behalf of society's many and varied consumers (voters). Voting arrangements do not allow large numbers of individuals to express their different preferences for the types of goods and services to be purchased by the public sector. Instead, public procurement officials and agencies have discretion in interpreting the "public interest" and in obtaining "good value for money". On this basis, the possibility arises that inefficiencies and failures in public procurement markets are *policy-created* and a preferred outcome.

5.4 DOES ECONOMIC THEORY OFFER ANY GUIDELINES FOR EC POLICY?

The market failure approach suggests that state intervention is required whenever private markets are failing to work properly. Applied to public procurement, inefficiencies and market failures arise where procurement officials restrict entry to the market. Examples include preferential purchasing favouring national or local suppliers, or the limited circulation of information on government contracts to a restricted list of selected firms. In which case, market failure arises on the buying side of the market. As a result, some public purchasing might be restricted to domestic industries which are monopolies or oligopolies involving substantial departures from the economists model of perfect competition. Within the EC, such industries include aerospace, coal, computers, iron and steel, power generation equipment, railway rolling stock and telecommunications.

Competitive markets are characterised by large numbers of relatively small buyers and sellers and free entry into, and exit from, the market. However, for some products such as defence equipment and telecommunications, the government is the major or only buyer, so that it has considerable power (that is, monopsony). It has to choose a product, select a contractor and negotiate a contract. Its purchasing decisions can determine the size and structure of an industry; it can restrict entry and prevent exits; its product choices can determine technical progress; and its regulatory rules can affect prices and profitability. Even this description of public purchasing conceals the complexities and transactions costs involved in acquiring information about products and suppliers, organising competitions, bargaining with contractors and then writing, monitoring and enforcing contracts.

Some of the elements in public purchasing decisions are outlined in Table 5.2. For simplicity, the market structure is restricted to the contrasting cases of competitive and bilateral monopoly markets. The Table shows the tendering arrangements, the choice criteria and the different types of contracts which can be awarded. For example, in competitive markets, governments can choose an open competition allowing any firm to bid for a contract or it can use selective tendering inviting bids from a limited number of firms from an approved list and of known reliability. Usually, with such competitions the product requirements are clearly specified and a fixed price-contract is awarded to the lowest bidder. However, with only one domestic supplier, the government has to enter into direct negotiations with a monopolist choosing between a fixed price, cost-plus or incentive contract. For example, where a government orders a project involving substantial risks and uncertainty extending over a number of years (for example, high technology defence equipment; Concorde), contractors are likely to require some form of cost-plus contract with the state bearing most of the risks (Hartley, 1990, Chapter 6).

120

Table 2
Public purchasing choices

Numbers of:					
Buyers	Market Sellers	Structure	Tendering	Criteria	Contracts
Large	Large → Competitive →		Open Competition, Selective Competition	Price or non price (e.g. design delivery)	Fixed price Cost-plus Incentive type
One (government)	One (monopoly) →	Bilateral (monopoly) →	Negotiation		

What are the implications of this analysis for EC policy on public procurement? Major elements of the market failure approach appear to have been incorporated into EC policy rules. EC policy aims to improve efficiency in public procurement by opening-up procurement markets, so allowing rival firms from other EC nations to bid for government contracts. This requires that national governments publicise information on their buying requirements and act as competitive buyers allowing firms from other EC nations to bid, so creating contestable markets. In other words, EC policy is designed to remove discrimination, protectionism, monopoly rights and anti-competitive behaviour by government buyers, so creating a "level playing field" in public procurement. Inevitably, problems arise in translating such aims and general principles into an actual operational policy.

5.5 POLICY FORMULATION: PROBLEMS AND PITFALLS

General economic principles on public procurement have to be converted into a set of EC rules and directives. There are problems of definition, exemptions, rules for competition, the eligibility of suppliers, minimum time periods for tendering and the criteria for awarding contracts.

Public sector contracting entities have to be defined so as to embrace a diversity of alternative public procurement arrangements and delivery systems for a variety of goods and services. For example, government purchasing might be undertaken centrally or locally or by special agencies or delegated to the private sector; and governments might buy goods and services directly from private firms or from publicly-owned companies, or activities might be undertaken "in-house", or licences can be awarded permitting firms to operate agreed services (for example, airlines; buses; taxis). Furthermore, all the goods and services to be covered by the EC directives have to be defined. However, the EC public procurement rules do not apply to contracts whose value falls below ECU 200,000 for supplies and services, and below ECU 5 million for works contracts (capital projects: EC 1989 a, p.103).

There are EC rules relating to open, restricted and negotiated purchasing procedures; as well as requirements for advertising contracts and announcing the results in the *Official Journal of the European Communities*. The criteria for awarding contracts are also specified as either the lowest price or the "most economically advantageous" tender which embraces such factors as delivery dates, running costs, quality, aesthetic and functional characteristics, spares, security of supplies as well as price. The policy is policed and enforced by the EC, with the ultimate resort to the European Court of Justice.

As with any public policy change, there will be gainers and losers and its ultimate social desirability will depend on whether the potential gainers could over-compensate the potential losers. Understandably, the potential losers will lobby for change and modification to reduce the penal effects of the policy. Firms and regions which have been protected from competition for government contracts (for example, national champions) will stress the likely "dire economic and social consequences" through job losses, the destruction of valuable human capital and the break-up of local communities (see Chapter 7). Here, economists can contribute by subjecting myths and emotion to critical evaluation and to an assessment of the available empirical evidence. However, vote-sensitive politicians might be persuaded that "something must be done" to reduce the harm to be imposed on the potential losers (for example, more time is required to adjust to the new policy). The result might be a substantial modification of the aims of the EC policy on public procurement with adverse effects on the magnitude of the expected benefits.

Confronted with an EC policy seeking to liberalise public procurement, firms and agents in political markets are unlikely to be passive organisations. Instead, they are likely to respond and adjust to the policy and try to thwart its aims. It is not unknown for some responses to be unexpected and undesirable! Consider, for example, the various methods which public buyers and firms might use to thwart the aims of EC policy. Government purchasers might split large contracts into a series of smaller ones which fall below the EC minimum levels so that they do not have to be advertised throughout the EC. Or, public buyers might try to impose constraints on a contractor such as requirements to buy locally or to use local labour (EC 1989 b, p.13). Similarly, government might reject "abnormally low offers" as representing too great a risk of bankruptcy and contractor failure. And applying the criteria of the "most economically advantageous" tender allows substantial opportunities for buyers to exercise discretion in their choices (for example, good value for money and in the interests of public health and safety). Firms might also respond to efforts to open-up public procurement markets through collusive tendering, cartels, take-overs and mergers. Furthermore, they will demand that firms from outside the EC be excluded from competitions for EC government contracts. Of course, the EC has anticipated some of these responses by public buyers and by contractors and has tried to formulate appropriate rules and regulations. As a result, it often seems that the extensive and detailed EC directives on public procurement are designed to benefit Commission officials and lawyers rather than the Community's taxpayers.

5.6 CONCLUSION: AGENDA FOR ACTION

EC policy aims to remove discrimination in public procurement by allowing rival firms from other EC nations to bid for government contracts. Estimates suggest substantial economic benefits, although these might have been exaggerated by those interest groups favouring and supporting the policy. At the same time, the potential losers from the policy will try to prevent, modify or slow-down the process of change. Here, the EC Commission has a continuing and important role in providing information to politicians and taxpayers on the costs of protectionism in public procurement. The Commission needs to be vigilant and active in repeatedly reminding its member states of the extra costs involved in using government contracts to support national champions.

There are two further areas for EC policy initiatives. First, the issue of relations with non-EC nations and the opportunities for their firms to bid for EC government contracts. There are worries of a "fortress Europe" policy which would remove an important source of competitive stimulus for EC producers. Second, there are extensive opportunities for "opening-up" public procurement in EC defence equipment markets. UK evidence suggests that introducing competition for defence equipment projects leads to cost savings of between 10% and 70% (Cmnd 344, 1988, vol.1, p.37). Of course, efforts to "open-up" EC defence equipment markets will be met with howls of protest from scientists and producer groups likely to lose from the policy. They will support their case by stressing the prospects of a massive brain drain, and the loss of both high technology and national independence. Usually, such howls of protest are an indicator of the degree of protectionism in public procurement.

NOTES

1. This paper is based on a research project funded by the Leverhulme Trust: the usual disclaimers apply.

REFERENCES

Catinat, M. 1989, The large Internal Market under the microscope: problems and challenges in Jacquemin, A. and Sapir, A. (eds), *The European Internal Market,* Oxford University Press, Oxford.
Cecchini, P., 1988, *The European Challenge 1992:* The Benefits of a Single European Market, Wildwood House, Aldershot.

Cmnd 344, 1988, *Statement on the Defence Estimates*, HMSO, London.

EC 1989 (a) *Public Procurement in the Excluded Sectors*, Bulletin of the European Communities, Supplement 6/88, Commission of the European Communities, Luxembourg.

EC 1989 (B), *Public Procurement: Regional and Social Aspects*, Commission of the European Communities, Brussels, July.

Hartley, K. 1990, *The Economics of Defence Policy*, Brasseys, London.

6 The community budget and 1992

T. Georgakopoulos and T. Hitiris

6.1   INTRODUCTION

A basic aim of the Treaty of Rome is 'to establish the foundations for an ever closer union among the European peoples', an economic and political union. To reach this objective the member states must gradually confer to Community institutions certain of their functions and activities and the powers to operate them. These will be the common targets which will be pursued by common policies at costs shared by all the participants. A policy instrument for the implementation of common policies at the level of the Community is the Budget which in the past has caused many problems to the member states. After many years of troubling budgetary difficulties and acrimonious disputes, the European Community finally agreed in 1988 the outline of the functions of the European Budget and its structure of revenues and expenditures until 1992. However, the budgetary problems have not been solved. After 1992, enhancement of competition in the single market and the move towards monetary integration are expected to have profound effects on certain regions, population groups and even member states. Hence the European Budget will be called upon to play a more substantial role in the allocation of costs and benefits of integration for two main reasons: first, this will be required for upward convergence, cohesion and growth of the European Community as a whole. Second, in the pursuit of common goals the member states will lose the use of some of their policy instruments, such as interest rates, money supply and exchange rates, and will have constraints imposed on the use of others, such as national budgets, so that a centrally directed common budget will be required to assist them reach their objectives during the process of integration.

After a brief description of the EC Budget and the problems it caused during the first 30 years of the Community's life, we examine its functions, the appropriate fiscal instruments for pursuing these functions and the proper sources of financing them after the single European market is established.

6.2 MAIN BUDGETARY DEVELOPMENTS IN THE EC

In accordance with the terms of the Treaty of Rome, the EEC Commission was given an operational budget and the task of administering two funds, the Social Fund and the Agricultural Fund. Following the 'Merger Treaty' of the EEC, the EURATOM and the European Coal and Steel Community (ECSC) in 1987, their budgets were brought together under the Community Budget. Initially, the Budget was specific; the revenues consisted of fixed financial contributions made by the member states on an agreed scale, and the expenditures were directed to clearly specified activities (Articles 199–209), under the constraint that 'the revenue and expenditure shown in the budget shall be in balance' (Article 199). Hence, this Budget was not substantially different from the budgets of other international organisations, which usually have more moderate aims than those of the European Community.

In 1970, in accordance with the provisions of the Treaty (Article 201), the Council decided to replace gradually the financial contributions of member states to the Community Budget by revenues from appropriately allocated 'own resources' directly paid to the Community as of right. An advantage of this new system of Community finances is that the Commission gained a certain degree of power by loosening its economic dependence on the member states which, moreover, cannot default on payment (Shackleton, 1990). However, at the current phase of European integration the Community Budget is based on narrow foundations and continues to remain relatively insignificant in size. To a large extent, the EC Budget is still functioning as 'public expenditure

127

estimates', an account of revenues from specific resources and expenditures for specific purposes, in *ex-post* balance as required by the Treaty. Until very recently, the structure of the Budget was as follows:

a) *Revenues*
1. Customs revenue from the application of the Common Customs Tariff (CCT) on goods imported from third countries.
2. Variable import levies on imports of agricultural products from third countries arising under the Common Agricultural Policy.
3. A certain proportion of each member state's Value Added Tax (VAT) base, calculated on a common basis, as an additional and more secure source of budgetary 'own resources' revenue.

b) *Expenditures*
Expenditures from the Community budget are in the form of direct payments to recipients in individual member states or to countries outside the EC. *Allocated* expenditure is that which can be attributed to individual member states; it currently accounts for more than 67 per cent of the total. The remaining, called *unallocated* expenditure, goes either to recipients outside the Community, for example, as aid to developing countries, or to research and administrative outlays at the headquarters. Frequently problems and disputes emerge in the Community between the Council and the European Parliament from the classification of budgetary expenditure as compulsory or non-compulsory. Compulsory is 'expenditure necessarily resulting from the Treaty or from acts adopted in accordance therewith' (Article 203). The Parliament has the power to determine only the non-compulsory expenditure, and only within pre-specified limits.

The relative shares in total expenditure of the the various economic sectors to a large extent reflect the areas of active Community policy. Thus the highest proportion of the Community budget is spent on agriculture via the European Agricultural Guidance and Guarantee Fund (EAGGF), most of it as compulsory expenditure under the Guarantee section for the policy of price support for agricultural commodities. Expenditures under the Regional, Social and other Funds aim at improvement of the economic conditions either in disadvantaged regions or for disadvantaged categories of people. It is assumed that expenditure from these Funds constitutes a supplement to, and not a substitute for, similar expenditures incurred by the national governments of the member states. The expenditure on energy, industry, transport, research, and development aid has remained low.

The allocation of payments to and receipts from the Budget are different for each member state and therefore, besides its main objective which is the financing of the implementation of agreed common policies, the Community Budget functions as an instrument of income redistribution between the member states. The Commission argues that the budgetary costs and benefits (the budgetary incidence) per country cannot be assessed accurately and are not a factual reflection of the costs and benefits of membership. Therefore, provided gross injustices do not occur, they should not be assessed or published. Nevertheless, the budgetary incidence of the EC Budget has caused problems which for a long time led to sharp disputes between the members of the Community (Hitiris, 1988). The UK in particular complained repeatedly that it consistently contributed to the Budget the most and benefited the least. At the same time, problems in the EC's domestic and the international markets necessitated increases in compulsory expenditure which led the Community to financial crises:

1. *The UK budget rebate.* The basic problems of the impact of the Community Budget on the UK were debated even before accession in 1972 (HM Treasury, 1982). When the UK joined the Community, it accepted the existing system of budgetary finances, but it was agreed that during a transitional period its contributions to budgetary costs would rise gradually from 8.64 per cent in 1973 to 18.92 per cent in 1977. It became, however, obvious from early on that under the existing system of Community finances the UK's contribution to the Community Budget would be rising despite its low growth performance. Hence, the special arrangements governing the UK contributions were extended for two more years with the understanding that from 1980 the UK would be fully subject to the Community budgetary system. Moreover, at the insistence of the UK government, the Dublin Summit (1975) reached agreement on a Correction Mechanism designed to limit the gross contribution of countries in situations similar to that of the UK. However, soon after the agreement it became clear that the Correction Mechanism was inadequate and that from 1980 the UK would be, relatively to its per capita income, the biggest net contributor to the Budget. Hence the UK government, in

accordance with supporting documents of the Treaty of Accession, demanded a large cut in its contribution, claimed that a case of 'unacceptable situations' had arisen and that 'the very survival of the Community would demand that the institutions find an equitable solution'.

After repeated negotiations, the principle of compensating the UK for excess payments was accepted in 1980, when it was agreed that it would get back a fixed refund, approximately equal to two thirds of its own contribution. A new agreement reached at the Fontainebleau summit in June 1984 cut the UK's budgetary contribution by 66 per cent of the difference between its share of VAT payments and its percentage share of Community expenditure. The agreement attempted to settle once-for-all the problem of budgetary imbalance between the member countries on a longer-term basis by stating explicitly that 'any Member State sustaining a budgetary burden which is excessive in relation to its relative prosperity may benefit from a correction at the appropriate time'.

2. *Budgetary crises.* The 1970 agreement to assign a new source of finance to Community 'own resources' set a ceiling for members' contribution of 1 per cent of the VAT base. But delays in the introduction of the VAT in some EC countries meant that the replacement of all member states' financial contributions by VAT payments was not completed before 1980. In the meanwhile, budgetary expenditures kept rising and, after two years of operating the new system, the ceiling of 1 per cent was reached, with the implication that the Community had exhausted its finances before fulfilling its legal obligations. A new ceiling of 1.4 per cent was set at the Fontainebleau summit, and came into force on 1st January 1986. The new agreement provided that, under certain conditions, by a new unanimous decision of the Council and after ratification by the member states in accordance with national procedures, the ceiling could be raised to 1.6 per cent from the 1st January, 1988. However, with expenditure exceeding revenue, the financial crisis continued. Hence by intergovernmental agreement the Community's budgetary resources were temporarily increased further to an implicit level of 2.2 per cent of VAT revenues.

In an attempt to solve the Budget's financial crisis on a longer term basis the Fontainebleau agreement introduced 'budgetary discipline', a check procedure on the growth of budget expenditure. Accordingly, the

Council early on in the financial year has to establish in collaboration with the Commission a 'reference framework' setting the maximum level of expenditure which it considered it must adopt to finance Community policies during the following financial year. An additional constraint was also imposed; it was that the net expenditure relating to agriculture, calculated on a three-yearly basis, should increase less than the rate of growth of the own resources base. The Commission was required to observe these limits when making its draft budget proposals. If ministers agreed to any measures which threaten to result in the budgetary limit being exceeded, the Commission had the power to suspend it (EC, 1984 and 1986). However, this mechanism for reducing the growth of expenditure had not taken into consideration events which were outside the Community's control and had detrimental effects on the budget.

In the first half of 1986 the dollar fell by approximately 11 per cent and thus the ECU appreciated, increasing the cost of EC export subsidies. Moreover, the limits set by the Budget proved ineffective to stop agricultural support prices from rising and CAP guarantee expenditures continued to expand. As a consequence, the sums allocated to agriculture were rapidly depleted, exports ceased and the Community was forced to hang on to its food mountains with associated increases in storage expenditure. On the 'own resources' side, customs revenues and import levies declined as the value of imports fell because of a substantial fall in the price of oil, while at the same time, due to a general decline in economic activity, the VAT 'take' was not rising sufficiently to make up the difference. Thus the Community faced another budgetary crisis. The Commission came up with a temporary solution involving the introduction of 'creative accounting', that is of deferring payments until the next year, when it was hoped that the situation might have improved. But this device did not work as expected and half way through the financial year the Budget came apart and the Commission requested more emergency funds. These became available by intergovernmental agreements, and thus the final outcome was a budget much larger than the draft budget which the Council had rejected a few months earlier as being excessive. Nevertheless, in September 1986 the Commission released figures showing that the Community budget, agreed only two months earlier, was unworkable.

At the beginning of 1987 the Commission came up with the proposal

131

that the Community Budget should rise by 30 percent from its current level by the end of 1992. To ensure that the farm policy does not swallow up the extra funds, the Commission proposed that the size of the Budget should determine the extent of agricultural spending. This would involve the introduction of 'budgetary stabilisers', that is of set limits for the guarantee section of expenditure on agriculture determined by the size of existing stocks of output and current prices in the markets of the Community. The expectation was that the overall farm budget would increase by no more than the natural, annual increase in Community revenue, which was estimated to be about 2 percent in real terms.

By June 1987 the Community finances reached a new crisis. The Commission's original plans to effect large savings through CAP price support curbs and other measures were all but destroyed by the determination of member states' governments to preach austerity, but secure the best deal for their own agricultural sectors. The net result was that the Community once again ran out of money. With no other realistic alternative in sight, the Commission estimated that either the VAT contribution should be raised from 1.4 to 1.9 per cent or the Community would be unable to meet its commitments and avoid a new large deficit. At the same time the Parliament made known that it would no longer be prepared to put up with creative accounting measures designed to delay the Community's day of reckoning. Thus, it became clear that the Community was in urgent need of a saner and fairer budget system to enable it to meet its Treaty obligations regarding common policies and to pursue the objectives of integration. The need for reform finally reached consensus.

6.3   RECENT DEVELOPMENTS

The issues relating to the European Budget are economic, political and historical and involve a number of questions relating to national sovereignty and the delegation of power to supra-national authorities. The question the partners in the EC have had to face since the early 1970s was whether the Community should develop like other federal entities. This problem was examined by the MacDougall Committee which emphasised in its Report (EC, 1977) that no sufficient 'political homogeneity' existed to justify Community provision of public goods.

There was, however, a distinct sense of common destiny that differentiated the countries in the Community from those outside which could support a slow move towards fiscal federalism. Three stages of federal and economic integration were envisaged:

(a) Pre-federal integration, with a Community public sector taking up 2–2½ per cent of Community GDP;
(b) Federation with a small Community public sector, 5–7 per cent of GDP;
(c) Federation with a large Community public sector, 20–25 per cent of GDP.

However, the immense political implications of adopting a federal objective and the fact that the MacDougall Report was published at a time of serious economic problems for the members of the EC and the world economy, meant that its recommendations were never implemented.

The Community's target of 'harmonious development of economic activity' suggests that the Community Budget has an important role to play in the process of integration. Nevertheless, problems with the Community Budget do exist, because, although at this stage of integration it is small, it certainly has inter-state income redistribution effects which cannot be ignored. The net budgetary transfers to the least developed smaller members, Greece, Ireland and Portugal, amount currently (1990) to approximately 5 per cent of their GDP. Harmonious development does not, of course, mean equality of performance. However, convergence at a higher level of performance might be a requirement for harmonious development, as are competition on equal terms and balance in the spatial distribution of costs and benefits. The last is a very important target for the EC which should become the objective of a larger and more ambitious Community Budget with national contributions based closer to progressivity and the ability to pay.

Towards this end, further budgetary reforms were undertaken in conjunction with changes in the Common Agricultural Policy in preparation for 1992. The Commission pointed out that in the single market the Budget should gear expenditures towards the assistance of low income areas and that the resources available under the present system of finance are inadequate for meeting this objective, even after

133

the intended raising of the ceiling on the Community's share of VAT from 1.4 to 1.6 per cent. The Commission therefore proposed a reform of EC finances based on the introduction of a further source of revenue which would augment the Community's own resources. The basis of this supplementary resource would be provided by the difference between the GNP of each country and its VAT assessment. In this way the members' contributions will be related to their actual ability to pay. Following the introduction of the fourth source of revenue, the Community's share of VAT could be reduced to 1 per cent.

Consequently, the origin of own resources entered in the EC Budget is now:

(i)   agricultural levies and sugar duties;

(ii)   customs duties;

(iii)   the application of a rate of 1.4 per cent to value-added tax revenues determined in a uniform manner according to Community rules. The assessment base for VAT should not exceed 55 per cent of the gross GNP at market prices of each member state, measured in a uniform way on the basis of a Commission Directive; in this way the high-consumption, low-income member states would not be unreasonably overcharged;

(iv)   the application of a rate based on the difference between each member states's GNP and its harmonised VAT base for an overall ceiling of 1.4 per cent of GNP maximum, to be reached gradually by 1992.

The new arrangements ensured that the conclusions of the Fontainebleau Council on the correction of budgetary imbalances remain applicable. Compensation to the UK will be financed on the basis of a GNP scale (EC, 1988a).

The reorganisation of the system, which is expected to increase the volume of finances by about 15 per cent annually in real terms, has been supplemented by measures to instil greater budgetary discipline. Therefore it will be linked to reforms of Community policies. In particular, there will be:

(i)   New guidelines for agricultural expenditure, binding on the member states: the rate of increase in Guarantee expenditure on agriculture must not exceed 74 per cent of the rate of increase in

134

Community gross national product;

(ii) A legally binding limit on agricultural production covered by the Common Agricultural Policy; and

(iii) Annual expenditure stabilisers on a product-by-product basis the implementation of which will be supervised by the Commission. Consequently, the proportion of farm spending in the Budget is expected to decline from two-thirds to 56 per cent by 1992, with a guaranteed rise in the share of the structural funds (Regional Fund, Social Fund and Guidance section of the European Agricultural Guidance and Guarantee Fund) to over a quarter of the Budget.

The new system of Community finances were approved by Council, with the addition of an amendment introduced by the Parliament that the own resources paid by each member state should reflect the 'relative wealth and income of the citizens' rather than its 'ability to contribute'. The Parliament also asked the Commission to submit a proposal for the introduction of a new levy in the form of a Community tax to replace one or more national taxes. Finally, the European Parliament, the Council and the Commission signed an inter-institutional agreement (July 1989) setting out for each of the years 1988 to 1992 detailed financial perspectives representing annual expenditure ceilings and budgetary discipline (Table 1). The Commission was also asked to present before the end of 1991 a report on the application of the new budgetary system and the amendments which need to be made to it in the light of experience (EC, 1988). Barring surprises, the budget problem has been solved until 1992. The European Council has not decided what the Community Budget should be like after 1992.

The new system started to be implemented for the 1989 Budget and the Commission stated that 'for the first time in several years, the Community will have a budget based on an amount of available own resources sufficient to finance all its political, economic and social objectives' (Bulletin EC, 1989/6). On the expenditure side, the situation was also eased by the strengthening of the dollar which pushed world agricultural prices up and thereby reduced demands on the Community budget. The new budget also revealed the implementation of structural changes with a significant increase in non-compulsory expenditures (+20 per cent) and virtually no growth in compulsory expenditures.

Table 1

Financial Perspectives 1988–1992 commitment appropriations
in million ECUs

	1988	1989	1990	1991	1992
1. Agricultural Guarantees	27,500	28,613	30,700	31,350	32,000
2. Sructural Operations	7,790	9,522	11,555	13,160	14,630
3. Multiannual Allocations	1,210	1,708	2,071	2,340	2,610
4. Other Policies	2,103	2,468	2,729	2,940	3,050
5. Repayments and Admin.	5,741	5,153	4,930	4,390	3,900
6. Monetary Reserves	1,000	1,000	1,000	1,000	1,000
Total	45,344	48,464	52,985	55,180	57,190
Compulsory Expenditure %	74.40	69.70	66.90	64.60	63.10
Own Resources as % of GNP	1.14	1.13	1.15	1.16	1.16

Notes: Current prices 1988–89; constant prices 1990–92.
Source: EC Inter-institutional Agreement (June 1988)/91), as adopted in April 1989/97.

6.4 THE ROLE OF THE BUDGET IN THE SINGLE MARKET AFTER 1992

Discussion on the role of a budget involves examination of three separate but highly interrelated questions: i) What are the proper functions to be carried out by the public body whose budget is being analysed ? In the present case this means an examination of the role of the Community's central authority *vis-à-vis* the governments of the member states. ii) What are the appropriate policies and activities involving budgetary arrangements to be used for accomplishing these functions? This question refers to the size and structure of the expenditure side of the budget. iii) What are the means of financing the budget which are compatible with, and can further promote, the goals pursued by the public body? This question refers to appropriate structure of the revenue side of the budget.

In this section we shall analyse these three questions with respect to the European Budget after 1992, drawing on the theory of multi-layer governments and the practice followed in existing federations. For, although the EC still displays insufficient 'political homogeneity' and is not at present, and it may not be for a long time, ripe for a political federation, the interdependencies between the participating economies are already so great, and will be even greater after 1993, that the situation is akin to an 'economic' federation. As Oates (1972) has put it, a federation exists whenever public sector decision making is both centralised and decentralised and choices of the provision of public services made at each level are determined by the demand for these services by the residents within the appropriate jurisdictions. This appears to be the situation in the EC. Political and legal considerations clearly play a substantial role in the determination of both the functions to be allocated to each level of government and of the policies and activities, as well as the means of finance to be employed in each case. For, besides forming binding constraints, such factors affect the degree of a society's homogeneity and coherence which are major determinants of the proper allocation of functions between the various layers of government. Therefore, in drawing our principles from the theory of federal finance and the experience of actual federations, account will be taken of these political and legalistic differences as well as of the low degree of coherence in the 'European' society as compared with the situation in actual federations.

6.4.1 The Functions of the EC Institutions After 1992

In a multi-tier government the allocation of the functions among the various levels is a constitutional question. The economist can contribute when forming or revising the constitution, by indicating the level of government which, on economic grounds, is more appropriate to carry out each function. The Treaty of Rome, which is the EEC's founding constitution, was based on the pluralist approach to economic integration according to which 'the international organisation has no real will of its own and no power to create a new political entity apart from the wishes of its members' (Pentland, 1973, p. 51). Therefore the Treaty of Rome does not give much power to the EEC's institutions. In contrast to the pluralist approach, which advocates a minimum degree of integration for the attainment of certain limited economic and political objectives, the federalist approach to integration involves the formation of a supra-national authority and powerful institutions to regulate the behaviour of the constituent states and to assume many of their sovereign rights, duties and obligations. Although neither pluralism nor federalism have been explicitly adopted as the guidelines of the EC nor do they receive the unanimous support of its constituent states, the role of EC institutions has been somewhat strengthen by the Single European Act (SEA, EC Commission, 1985). Moreover, these institutions would probably require and demand more power, if they are to carry out their functions in the new environment created after 1992. It is therefore interesting to review the salient features of federal finance and try to see the extent to which they are relevant in the case of the European Community.

A generally accepted proposition in the theory of federal finance is that the central government is the appropriate level of government to look after the goal of stabilisation. In contrast, member states are severely constrained in this respect by the high degree of openness of their economies which would cause large leakages and render national stabilisation policy ineffective (Oates 1972, Musgrave 1969). Somewhat parallel conditions are found in the EC. Although the degree of openness of the EC member states may not be as high as in a federation, it is today high enough, and it will rise further after 1992, to hinder severely the effectiveness of any member's stabilisation policy. Some degree of involvement of the central institutions will therefore be necessary in the area of stabilisation policy. The crucial question that arises here is whether it is necessary to give to the EC institutions the powers and the means to look after the goal of stabilisation or whether we should simply restrict their role to a coordination of the member countries' stabilisation policies. The answer to this question depends on the course chosen by the EC members for their integration. However, we could perhaps distinguish between two different situations: (1) the one existing before full monetary union, where member countries' exchange rates will be fixed within relatively narrow margins, but still they could be adjusted when necessary by realignments of the central rates; and (2) the one after full monetary integration with a central monetary authority and a common currency. In the former situation the economic (and political) structure of the union is quite distinct from that of a federation, since each member state has the responsibility of looking after its balance of payments, while the second situation is more akin to a federation. Members need not, and in fact cannot, look after external disequilibria as their imbalances are financed by the common currency. Therefore in the case of non-federation there is much scope for leaving the stabilisation function with the individual member states, the only role to be given to the EC institutions being that of coordinating the policies to make them more effective in view of the increasing degree of interdependence among the economies of the union. After full monetary integration, however, member states will not have to finance their balance of payments imbalances themselves. Nevertheless, differences in productivities among the various regions of the Community will tend to cause different levels of growth and therefore appropriate policies need to be instituted to deal with diverging demand and incomes in the member states as well as with the overall growth level of the Community. As a result the role of the EC institutions in the area of stabilisation must be strengthened progressively and member states' stabilisation policies must be more closely coordinated, with some functions progressively delegated to the European Budget.

Concerning the question of equity and income distribution, again there exists a presumption in favour of centralisation in federal states, since a decentralised aggressive redistributory policy may be self-defeating (Oates, 1972). Similar considerations seem to apply in the case of the EC, but two fundamental differences must be taken into account. First, in a political federation, the community is presumably more coherent and homogeneous in terms of preferences for redistribution. In fact, in the case of the EC the whole notion of equity may be different from that in existing federations. The fundamental principle of equal treatment of equals, which means that the public sector must treat all economic agents in similar position equally, may not be applicable to the same extent here. In federal states, it is the constitution, expressing the will of the people, that encompasses this principle. In the EC, neither the Treaty of Rome nor the Single European Act (SEA) contain such a principle. The aim of the Community, according to these Treaties, is to promote a harmonious development in the economies of the member countries and an increase in the welfare of their peoples. There does not seem to exist as yet any notion of equity among individuals belonging to different member states. In fact, in view of the divergent preferences among individuals in the different states concerning the role of the public

139

sector and its scope for redistribution, it seems rather improbable that such a clause will emerge yet from the inter-governmental conference which will assemble in December 1990 to consider constitutional revisions of the Treaties. This is however a political question and will not be pursued further here. Second, the mobility of productive factors in the EC is much less than in a political federation – arising, for example, from language barriers etc. – so that member states may successfully pursue different redistributive policies without causing wide inefficiencies in the location of production factors, especially labour.

The above reasons seem to suggest that, for a long time to come and until circumstances are ripe for some sort of political federation in Europe, the role of the European Budget in the area of income redistribution will be more restricted than in actual federations. Rather than providing for inter-personal equity to comply with the principles of horizontal and vertical equity, however interpreted, the role of the European Budget must perhaps be restricted to that of ensuring that each member state has a fair share in the net costs and benefits of economic integration; that is there is inter-state equity but subject to the requirement for convergence in the Community. On distributive grounds therefore, the revenue and expenditure sides of the budget must be judged on the basis of the inter-country redistributive role. After all, even in existing federations, the federal government tends to provide for such inter-state equity via grants-in-aid rather than to affect income distribution among citizens throughout the federation. To this end, the federal budget may have to redistribute income among the union member countries for three reasons: i) to counterbalance undesirable redistribution caused by the existence of discriminatory protective instruments, such as the common external tariff and the variable levy system, or common policies, such as the CAP; ii) to arrive at a fair share in the benefits of economic integration among the member states (inter-state equity); iii) to pursue the objective of convergence and harmonious development among the member states in the Community.

It is well known that protective measures such as tariffs and variable levies redistribute income from consumers to domestic producers in the importing country. When policy instruments provide for differential treatment of imports according to source, as is the case in economic unions, a redistribution of income from consumers in the importing country to producers in the exporting country takes place

(Georgakopoulos 1986, Ardy 1988). Similar effects arise from the price support policies of the CAP which transfer income from domestic consumers (and probably foreign producers) to domestic producers. If this automatic redistribution is deemed undesirable, budgetary counter-transfers can be used to effect an appropriate distribution. Such transfers can also be used to redistribute income among member countries, if the distribution of the net benefits of integration arrived at via the market price mechanism is not deemed satisfactory on inter-state equity grounds or appears to work against convergence. Grants-in-aid can be unconditional in the former two cases, while in the last case matching grants are more desirable since such grants can better promote the goal of convergence.

Finally, in terms of allocative efficiency, there still exists scope for activity by the federal government, mainly in situations where federal public goods, wide externalities or unexploited economies of scale are involved. But, on allocative efficiency grounds, the case is stronger for lower level government activity, since local government units can better adjust the provision of public goods to the particular preferences of the constituent population. The scope for centralisation here depends on the extent of externalities, the existence and the size of economies of scale, and the degree of homogeneity of preferences. In Europe the economies of most member countries are large enough, and the government sectors so advanced that probably there are not many unexploited economies of scale. More centralisation may, in fact, meet with diseconomies rather than with economies of scale, though of course there may be some activities, for example, defence or protection against terrorism, where centralisation of public provision may be advocated. Some degree of centralisation seems also to come up on account of externalities, again in areas such as defence and protection against terrorism, where externalities are perhaps substantial. Externalities are also present if the existing budgetary arrangements cause redistribution between the member states (which, as we have seen, is what is happening in the EC). In this case, familiar principles from federal finance support the shift from lower- to higher-level governments (Musgrave 1969, Oates 1972, Wildasin 1990).

In contrast to the economies of scale case, the demand for public services is perhaps much more diversified among the member states of the EC than among the member states of a federation and this, of course, supports decentralisation of provision. The wider divergence in the pattern of demand for public services in the EC arises from the fact that preferences and average incomes diverge much more among the EC member states than among states of a federation. In conclusion, on allocative efficiency grounds, there is much scope for decentralisation in the provision of public services in the EC, but centralisation may be considered in the case of certain public goods.

6.4.2 EC Policies and Activities Involving Budgetary Payments

The first fact to be pointed out with respect to the expenditure activities of the EC institutions is the relatively small size of their operations. Total EC expenditure in 1988 amounted to only 1.14 per cent of the Community GNP and is planned to increase to 1.16 per cent by 1992 (Table 1), a ratio much smaller than the one recommended for the Pre-federal integration stage by the MacDougall Report. Compared to national budgets, which range between 33 per cent in Portugal to 58 per cent in Denmark and a Community average of 44 per cent, the EC Budget is small and inadequate to play any substantial role in the Community economies. A second drawback of the expenditure side of the Budget is that it is still dominated by the Guarantee section of the EAGGF, while the share of the structural funds remains small. In fact, the structure of the budgetary policies and expenditures to a large extent still reflect the political balance and the economic interests of the founder members of the Community with agriculture being the financially dominant common policy. Hence, countries with large agricultural sectors still benefit from the budget, at the cost of other member countries, such as the UK. The increase in the share of the structural funds is a deliberate attempt to improve this situation.

The Common Agricultural Policy (CAP) has been used to achieve both an economic objective in the production of agricultural commodities (some unspecified degree of self-sufficiency) and a social objective (a fair income for the farmers). Hence the Community Budget still is a sort of a consumption budget with a relatively small contribution to investment and the restructuring of the economy of the member states. A considerable improvement took place after the recent decision to double the size of the structural funds by 1992 (entries 2 and 3 in Table 1). More changes are probable if agreement is reached at the Uruguay round of GATT negotiations for staged liberalisation of trade in agricultural

142

products. In this case the Community would have to apply policies in support of agricultural incomes, which should be neutral with respect to international trade. One way to achieve this objective under neutrality is via direct income transfers to farmers from the Budget. The role of grants from the EC institutions will therefore most probably increase after 1992. They will be called upon to promote inter-state equity in the sense of achieving a desirable distribution of the net benefit from integration, with due account given to convergence. They will also be the appropriate means of implementing some of the EC policies in a more neutral way. It is therefore interesting to look at such grants more closely.

Federal government grants are usually classified into two broad categories: conditional and unconditional. Conditional grants are those for which the grantor determines, to a certain extent, the purpose for which the recipient is to use the funds. Unconditional grants are those which can be used by the recipient freely according to his own needs and priorities. Conditional grants can be either matching grants or non-matching. In the former case, which is used today for structural funds in the EC, the recipient government has to match each grant-unit received with a certain amount from its own resources, while in the latter case the recipient government does not have to contribute national financing. Matching grants have the advantage of ensuring that wasteful projects are avoided, a danger that is present when state governments can carry out projects for which another tier of government pays. In the case of the social policy functions of the CAP, the non-matching grant scheme seems to be more appropriate, even if the CAP is revised and direct income transfers to farmers are strengthened at the expense of price support policies and protection from foreign competition. This is so, among other reasons because the recipient of such direct support can be defined and identified, and this minimises the dangers of abusing the system.

Non-matching grants appear to be more appropriate in the context of the distribution objectives of the Budget. Indeed, if any grants are paid to state governments for purely redistributive purposes, so that a fairer distribution of the benefits from integration is achieved, the non-matching grant scheme is the most effective. The same is true of the stabilisation objectives, if stabilisation activities through fiscal means are finally transferred from state governments to the EC institutions.

6.4.3 The Finance of the Budget

The revenue side of the European Budget remains unsatisfactory. Before the introduction of the fourth 'own resource', revenues came exclusively from indirect taxes. Hence their effects on the member states were regressive and clearly accentuated income divergence between Community members. The introduction of the new source of revenue has made an improvement, but still the total contribution of each country to the European Budget is not proportional to national GNP and, therefore, does not promote convergence. Since a primary aim of the Community is more integration, for which economic convergence is necessary, it is essential that new and more appropriate and more progressive revenue sources are introduced. One long-term solution to this problem perhaps is to introduce a Community corporate income tax and/or a Community personal income tax on all European Community corporations and citizens. Looking at existing federations, a federal income tax is normally expected to play this role, but in the Community this would have to wait until political considerations are more ripe and the member states can proceed to some sort of more coherent political unity. In the meantime less ambitious solutions must be sought that will improve the revenue side of the European Budget in the medium term.

New sources which could be used as medium term solutions should have the following characteristics: first, they must be progressive with respect to GNP so that they promote convergence in the Community; and, second, they must concern highly mobile productive factors over which more than one member state's fiscal authorities may have a claim for tax revenues. Income from productive factors employed in a member country, with their owners residing in another member country seem to meet these criteria. On the two considerations, income from financial capital seems to be a most satisfactory source, since taxes on such income are probably progressive in terms of GNP, even if they are levied on a proportional nominal rate. Moreover, financial capital will perhaps be the most mobile factor in the Community after 1993. Two alternative or complementary sources of revenue seem to emerge here: i) The harmonised capital levy of 1 per cent, which has already been introduced in the member countries; and ii) A harmonised tax levied at a single rate on bank deposits, which is under consideration for introduction in all EC member countries as a national source of revenue.

The above two sources seem to be suitable for the medium term finance of the European Budget and can cover the Community needs for many years to come. Besides being progressive and, from the jurisdictional point of view, among the most inter-national, they also are easily identifiable low collection-cost sources, where fraud by both the taxpayers and the member states themselves is relatively difficult.

6.5 CONCLUSIONS

The European Community is moving towards Economic and Monetary Union (EMU) and some degree of political co-operation. This will solve certain problems in the Community but it will also create new problems particularly for the weaker regions which may be unable to follow the economic policies and the pace of growth of the advanced regions. A thorny question is whether EMU should entail central control of member-countries' budget deficits. One line of argument maintains that, if governments were free to borrow wildly, the EMU would not work. Therefore the planned EMU treaty (the details of which will be discussed at an inter-governmental conference which will be convened in December, 1990) should include clauses on central budgetary control. Political considerations may dictate, however, that the EMU treaty should limit its scope to recommending policy changes to any country whose borrowing is judged excessive, banning the financing of government deficits by printing national money and laying down specific conditions for granting assistance to member countries in difficulties. Therefore, the Community Budget will be called upon to play a more active role in Community economic policy for balanced growth and integration promoting convergence. This is a problem which the Community has not settled by the recent budgetary accords and it is likely that budgetary issues will be reopened as the Community progresses towards the single market. The present chapter has offered some ideas based on fiscal federation principles adapted for the case of the EC. For as long as the European Community remains an economic union of national states, the Community budget will have to play a complementary, yet progressively increasing, role to that played by the national budgets of the member states, with main objectives the promotion of integration and the fair distribution of its costs and benefits among the member states.

REFERENCES

Ardy, B. (1988),'The National Incidence of the European Community Budget', Journal of Common Market Studies, 26, pp. 401–29.

EC (1977), Report of the Study Group on the Role of Public Finance in European Integration, MacDougall Report, Brussels.

EC (1984), 'The Budget', Bulletin EC–6, 1984.EC (1986), The European Community's Budget, 4th edition, European Documentation, Luxembourg.

EC Commission (1985), 'Completing the Internal Market', White Paper from the Commission to the European Council, Document, Official Publications of the EC, Luxembourg.

EC (1988), 'Interinstitutional Agreement on budgetary discipline and improvement of the budgetary procedure', Annex III, Official Journal, no. L 185.

EC (1988a), 'Brussels European Council', Bulletin of the European Communities, 21, pp. 8–23.

Georgakopoulos, T. (1986), 'Greece in the European Communities: A View of the Economic Impact of Accession', The Royal Bank of Scotland Review, 150.

Hitiris, T. (1988), European Community Economics, Harvester-Wheatsheaf, Hemel Hempstead.

H M Treasury (1982), The European Community Budget: Net Contributions and Receipts, Economic Progress Report Supplement/ October.

Musgrave, R. A. (1969), Theories of Fiscal Federalism, Public Finance, 24, pp. 521–536.

Oates, W. E. (1972), Fiscal Federalism, Harcourt Brace Jovanovich, New York.

Pentland, C. (1973), International Theory and European Integration, Faber, London.

Shackleton, M. (1990), Financing the European Community, Chatham House Papers, The Royal Institute of International Affairs, Pinter Publishers, London.

Wildasin, D.E. (1990), 'Budgetary Pressures in the EEC: A Fiscal Federalism Perspective', Americal Economic Review, 80, Papers and Proceedings, pp.69–74.

7 1992: An Italian Perspective

Giovanni Palmerio

7.1 INTRODUCTION

The current pressure from some quarters to speed up the process of monetary integration in Europe by the creation of a European central bank and a single currency may be the result of a misplaced enthusiasm and a failure to appreciate some important differences in the EC members' economies. In this chapter it will be argued that a considerable degree of convergence in economic performance will need to be achieved if conditions in national economies are not to put such a strain on the process of monetary unification that will jeopardise its eventual achievement. The *1992* measures which seek to promote a more closely-knit EC economy through the medium of increased competition is one, but only one, step towards this necessary convergence. Other policies, specifically structural ones to deal with imbalances between countries and regions in Europe will be necessary. The most pressing in this respect are in the areas of employment and industrial development. There is in other words a need for some interventionist policies of the type that will increase the attractiveness to industry of areas such as Italy's Mezzogiorno both to offset any tendency for firms to relocate in the so-called core of the European economy and as well as to boost the performance of these areas.

Another reason why interventionist supply-side policies will be needed arises because the progressive monetary integration of the EC economies significantly reduces the freedom of national governments to pursue their own demand policies. Thus the requirement to peg, and later to fix, exchange rates in the EMS along with the increasingly liberalised financial markets in which capital can move freely will not only curtail national governments' control over interest rates but may also limit the size of budget deficits. Consequently supply-side employment and industrial policies will be the only way of tackling the existing and already serious unemployment problems in some parts of Europe. If the *1992* changes heighten the employment problems in some regions of the EC it becomes even more essential to formulate a coherent European strategy to ameliorate the resulting problems.

7.2 EMPLOYMENT AND PRODUCTIVITY

The Cecchini Report (1988) can be taken to express the dominant view of the effects of the *1992* measures on the EC economies. According to the Report, the abolition of various non-tariff barriers between EC countries will raise GDP by about 4.5 per cent and produce a fall in unemployment in the region of 1.5 per cent. There will be other favourable effects such as a reduction in the inflation rate and a relaxation of both the external and budget deficit constraints (see Introduction for details). These beneficial effects will be produced primarily as a result of the relaxation of the restrictions on trade in goods and services and on the flow of capital. Not only will the reduction of non-tariff barriers stimulate cooperation, forcing costs and prices down and causing the inefficient firms to close or be taken-over, there will also be major dynamic gains as the European market becomes increasingly concentrated and dominated by a few, large but highly competitive oligopolies. This may produce a Schumpeter-like competitive environment as these firms seek to gain advantages through product and process innovation. The larger size of the European firms and plants will also produce increasing returns to scale as the more sizeable market encourages businesses to adopt production methods that exploit unrealised scale economies. (But see James in this volume for an assessment of this view.)

It is this type of analysis that underlies the favourable results derived by Cecchini and his associates. However, although it may have some merit there are a number of areas where it is questionable, one of which is on the employment front. There are two possible scenarios here, neither of which augurs well for the future of employment in Europe in the medium term.

The first concerns the situation in which the rate of productivity growth differs between countries, which seems likely given the past experience of the EC economies. In this case an increase in the imbalances in economic activity will come about. Assuming that, with the exception of Spain, Portugal and Greece, wages in the EC countries grow at a similar rate those economies experiencing slower productivity rises will lose competitiveness. These countries will suffer a decline in exports and a rise in imports, with consequent problems for the balance of payments and employment. Attempts to regain their competitive position and to maintain domestic employment by devaluing the exchange rate will cause serious problems for the EMS, since its efficacy depends largely on the fact that there is confidence in the commitment to maintaining fixed rates. Exchange rate movements are a last resort policy and frequent realignments would, therefore, undermine the system by changing expectations.

The second possibility is that productivity rises at a fairly uniform rate throughout the EC, an effect that may be produced by the *1992* barrier removing measures which force enterprises across Europe to increase their efficiency. An upward acceleration in the productivity trend without an accompanying rise in the growth of output will only worsen the outlook for employment in Europe. During much of the 1970s and 1980s this is what has happened in Europe with the predicted employment results.

In both cases, therefore, the steps towards integration will produce an initial rise in unemployment, although the longer-run prospects may well be rather brighter. It is in this first phase of adjustment that structural policies are required. Moreover, if the regional distribution of employment is taken into account the conclusions become even more pessimistic. While it is very likely that at the end of the adjustment process after the *1992* shock new jobs will be created, it is not at all certain where they will be located. In Italy for instance it is probable that unless remedial action is taken rapidly the regional disparity between the North and the South will widen still further.

7.3 LIMITATIONS ON MACROECONOMIC POLICIES

One approach to the employment problem is to adopt the traditional, nationally based macroeconomic policies such as using interest rates and budgetary policy to affect the level of economic activity. However in practice, there are considerable limits on both the effectiveness and possibility of macroeconomic policy, see Chapter 3.

It was argued in Chapter 3 that monetary union – even the ERM – involved the elimination of Budget deficits. This is clearly a problem for countries like Belgium and Italy which have large structural deficits. Moreover, any attempt to eliminate deficits has implications for social expenditure and so the distribution of income. Hence it is worth examining the argument that past deficits are responsible for Italy's economic problems, such as they are in the land of Il Sorpano.

If we adopt a Keynesian framework, according to which real variables have a dominant role in determining the evolution of the economy, we have the well known phenomenon of crowding out. According to this theory, public expenditure crowds out private expenditure and thus slows down economic growth. Moreover, crowding out may also occur through a process whereby an excess of demand in the presence of a rigid supply leads to inflation and/or to a deficit of the balance of payments. It is naturally possible to evaluate, by means of more sophisticated analyses, the conditions that lead to crowding out, the extent to which it is likely to occur, "financial crowding out", whether crowding out and inflation may occur simultaneously, or if one tends to exclude the other.

Another important interpretation of the relation between public deficits and inflation is that of monetarists. The monetarist school maintains that public deficits and fiscal policies have a very limited impact on the level of economic activity and prices, unless they occur together with variations in the money supply. The exponents of the so called fiscal monetarism maintain that the huge expansion of the public deficits that occurred in most industrialised countries in the last decades forced governments to raise the money supply, and this leads to inflation; most vividly in Sargent and Wallace's unpleasant monetarist arithmetic. However, the separation between the central bank and the Treasury that has been in many countries shows that there is no automatic link between the growth of public deficit and money creation.

In the Unites States the Reagan Administration claimed to endorse economic policies reflecting these principles but, for political reasons, it never succeeded in reducing public expenditure. Instead of falling, the public deficit rose. However, it was financed mainly by issuing bonds rather than by creating money. As it is well known, this caused a very strong increase in interest rates.

In short, recent experience shows that, without reducing its public deficit, but rather raising it, the United States has succeeded in reducing its rate of domestic inflation; while Britain, which has had no public deficit since 1988, still has a high rate of inflation, higher than the Italian one, notwithstanding the Italian huge public deficit.

While the relation between public deficit, inflation and balance of payments deficit has been extensively analysed, that between public deficit and the long-term rate of growth of GNP and of productivity has been discussed to a much smaller extent. These relationships appear to be even more uncertain. Some work on this point can be found in documents produced by international institutions and in the debate on the economic situation in Italy. The idea most frequently mentioned is the following: public expenditure crowds out private expenditure. The former consists especially of current expenditure, and has a lower productivity than the latter. Therefore a high public deficit curtails the rate of growth of the economy. Moreover, public deficit leads to inflation, which in turn, to be kept in check, requires authorities to adopt restrictive monetary and tax policies that hit especially private investment. The final outcome is a slowing down of production, a rise of unemployment and a reduction of the rate of growth of GNP. For many authors this is the main explanation of the stagflation that occurred in Italy and in other industrialised countries in the Seventies. However, experience shows that economies without budget deficits may stagnate, while others with a high deficit may grow at a satisfactory rate. During the Seventies and Eighties, when its public deficit exploded, Italy changed from a labour-exporting country into a labour-importing country, while various areas in its Mezzogiorno (Southern part) achieved a wide-spread industrialisation.

An important point that is often left aside is the following: a public deficit represents a redistribution of resources away from some economic agents (groups of individuals, firms etc.) to others. It alters the personal distribution of income (rather than the functional one), and this is a point that economists do not discuss very much. Obviously, if public expenditure consists of consumption expenditure (or social expenditure) while private expenditure consists of investments, there is no doubt that a continuous expansion of the public deficit reduces long-term growth. However, albeit in some periods public and private expenditure may have the characteristics mentioned above, this does not always occur.

As it is well known, public expenditure may concern education, professional training, or infrastructures, which, albeit being unprofitable in the short run, and therefore would never be made by private agents, are nevertheless fundamental for long-term development. Moreover, a part of the redistribution of resources that occurs through the public deficit goes to enterprises, in the form of incentives, subsidies and so on. This may often favour non competitive enterprises, but it may also allow to create, restructure or consolidate enterprises that are competitive even from an international point of view, which would not have occurred without the initial public subsidy.

It is therefore difficult to draw a clear-cut conclusion on whether public deficits crowd out private expenditure. Moreover, even if the deficit does lead to crowding out, when analysing the final effect of a public deficit on the economy's rate of growth, one should always consider the reallocation of resources it generates within the private sector (between families and enterprises and among various enterprises).

It is worth underlining that, in practice, public deficit (that is budgetary policy), like monetary policy, is an instrument for redistributing resources and real income among various social groups, sectors and geographical areas.

Such a massive redistribution of resources cannot be analysed only at an aggregate level, because it occurs among the thousands of microeconomic units that constitute an economy. Therefore, the question is whether such a redistribution of resources raises the overall productivity of the economy or reduces it; which impact has this redistribution on the total volume of investments and on their productivity?

7.4 INTERVENTIONIST SUPPLY-SIDE POLICIES

In the previous section it has been argued that under a fixed exchange rate régime with liberalised capital markets the need to reduce budget deficits and co-ordinate monetary policies will severely curtail governments in the pursuit of independent macroeconomic policies. The achievement of satisfactory levels of employment will therefore require the use of other policy instruments, specifically the use of supply-side policies aimed at the labour market but also for raising productivity. There are in fact four main areas in which the state has an important role to play; they are in encouraging the growth of productivity, regulating the supply of labour, promoting domestic industry and protecting it against foreign competition.

7.4.1 Productivity growth and technical progress

In modern mixed economies the rate at which new technologies are introduced depends to a large extent on government decisions as well as those of private sector enterprises. This is because of the size and the influence of the public sector both as a direct employer and as an initiator and paymaster of programmes to restructure industry and train or retrain manpower. It is not altogether evident, therefore, that the *1992* programme will automatically raise productivity and even if it does the consequence could be a serious rise in the level of unemployment in the medium term, as has already been discussed. The state can therefore pursue a dual role with regard to technical progress: first by encouraging it but second by managing and regulating its rate and direction in order to ensure that it is employment generating.

The example of computers serves to illustrate the point. As labour-saving devices the adoption of computer technology will cause unemployment in some sectors of the economy. On the other hand, additional jobs are created within the computer industry, and the wider and more rapid their diffusion throughout the economy the greater their employment creating effects. The state can clearly influence these positive employment effects by encouraging the increasing use of computers in the public sector both in administration as well as in schools and other fields.

7.4.2 Reducing Labour Supply

One popularly supported approach to persistently high unemployment has been that of reducing the supply of labour by measures to encourage the growth of part-time employment or by reducing working hours.

Various EC governments have introduced such measures already. Some economists have pointed out that, while reducing the supply of economically active workers, these policies tend to stimulate the supply from previously inactive groups. This is especially true of the effects of introducing more part-time job opportunities on the supply of female labour. The final outcome may be either an increase or a fall in the aggregate supply of labour. Moreover, these measures could have a negative impact on the demand for labour if they raise firms' production costs. The most serious objection to reducing working hours is that a country which is exposed to foreign competition cannot do so without taking into account the policies adopted in other countries. If working hours fell more rapidly in one country than others the effect would be a significant rise in unit labour costs and a serious loss of competitiveness.

However, introducing part-time jobs and shortening working hours may contribute to reducing unemployment if these measures are carefully managed. The reduction of working hours for example can be introduced as the productivity of the economy rises. Within an increasingly integrated European market in which national employment measures are restricted it is also clear that there will have to be a common employment policy to regulate labour supply. No individual EC economy will be able to afford to step out of line with the rest of the community without adversely affecting competitiveness, unless productivity growth rates differ. On the other hand, even a common employment policy will not be sufficient for Europe to maintain its competitive position with Japan and other fast growing economies; for that other policies that affect industry and trade directly will be required.

7.4.3 Regional and Industrial Policies

An activist industrial policy after *1992* may operate in two main ways; first to encourage the development of European industry as a whole, with the aim of increasing its competitiveness *vis à vis* Japan *et al*, and second, to correct the various regional imbalances that exist in the EC and which may widen as a result of the single market programme. It is with respect to the latter case that industrial policy has a particularly important role especially in areas such as Southern Italy, the Mezzogiorno.

Today the economy of the Mezzogiorno suffers from a number of serious handicaps. Great distances separate enterprises which limits the achievement of external and scale economies and also isolates firms from their major markets. There is also a lack of specialisation in production and output has a relatively low technological content. To correct these deficiencies a successful industrial policy will have to improve both the organisation of industry and raise its technological level. Moreover, as industrialisation does not spread in a homogeneous way but tends to concentrate in certain areas industrial policy will need to be more geographically and sectorally specific. This is a major change from Italy's past approach which followed a policy that encouraged the diffusion of firms over the whole country. The problem of a more localised industrial policy of course is that imbalances are created within a region but these can always be corrected or mitigated by other policies.

Even if industrial policy pursues a development strategy based on local firms, it should also consider that large external firms represent a fundamental stimulus for the economy of Italy's Mezzogiorno. The relative weight that large external firms have in the economy of Southern Italy in terms of employment and output makes the future of industry in this area depend largely on their decisions both with respect to the existing plants and to new investments. Therefore, a new, active industrial policy should be based on external firms both for strengthening the industrial structure of the Mezzogiorno and for sustaining growth of local businesses. Big national firms from the Centre and the North of Italy, however, are currently engaged in strengthening their presence in European markets. In order to encourage them to invest in Southern Italy, the relevant comparative advantages should be created. Furthermore, Italy should try to attract foreign, non-EC multinationals to invest in its southern region.

The attraction of foreign multinationals into Europe has produced an important stimulus to competition in oligopolistic industrial markets, but their entry often occurs through merger with existing enterprises and therefore through investment in well developed and already prosperous areas. There is no guarantee that inward investment will benefit the poorer regions such as Southern Italy. Multinational investment can also take the form of the construction of new plants on greenfield sites in peripheral areas of the EC economy where there may be significant cost benefits. Examples of this include Japanese investment in Portugal, Greece and the North East of England. As yet the Mezzogiorno has not

155

benefitted from such new investment. The reasons seem to be the lack of cost advantages in the form of low labour costs, specific sectoral advantages (external economies), research centres or its geographical position in relation to other parts of the Community.

The introduction of automatic tax incentives may prove to be an easier and more effective way of encouraging inward investment. These measures are often more efficient than discretionary ones, which need considerable competence and efficiency in their administration. They also require a great deal of information that is often costly to obtain. Thus the discretionary measures require a preliminary investigation of the firm, the investment and so on, which is often time consuming and invariably encourages firms to overstate their needs.

However, in the near future it is likely that such investment will be stimulated less and less by means of financial incentives, since the Community authorities are increasingly taking a stricter line on measures which distort competition. In any case, the incentives that will be allowed for the Mezzogiorno will also be allowed, for the other poor regions of Europe. Many of these, according to statistical indicators, are less developed than Italy's Mezzogiorno, even if in practice they are more able to attract private investments because they have important advantages such as low labour cost.

In the Nineties therefore industrial policies should use automatic instruments to lower costs and encourage investment in areas such as Southern Italy. Discretionary incentives, to the extent they may be introduced, should be used to finance big projects on behalf of groups of firms, that are able to produce a strong regional impact and to minimize external diseconomies. But incentives, even if important, will not be sufficient to attract investments in the South of Italy. Other measures aimed at improving the infrastructure and, in general, creating a more favourable environment for business will have to be adopted. Industrial policy should also provide "real incentives" to firms, especially to small ones, by helping them in the marketing of their products, by giving them financial consulting, training manpower through a permanent education process and continuously bringing up-to-date their technical and professional knowledge.

On the wider question of the competitiveness of European industry as a whole the appropriate policy for the EC might be to adopt a strategic trade policy that protects its domestic industries. This is the familiar planned trade option. It might entail the negotiation of trade and commercial policies along the lines of the Voluntary Export Restrictions on motor vehicle imports agreed with the Japanese producers, extending them to other sectors that are particularly vulnerable to intensive foreign competition.

REFERENCE

Cecchini, P. (1988), 1992: *The European Challenge,* Willdwood House.

Index

159

160